The Faith We Sing

D1710158

Worship Planner

Abingdon Press
Nashville, Tennessee

THE FAITH WE SING
Worship Planner

Copyright © 2000 by Abingdon Press

This book is printed on acid-free, recycled paper.

ISBN 0-687-09056-3

Scripture quotations are from the New Revised Standard Version Bible, copyright © 1989 by the Division of Christian Education of the National Council of the Churches of Christ in the USA.

Manufactured in the United States of America

CONTENTS

INTRODUCTION

The Faith We Sing Worship Planner is exactly what the title suggests: a resource for helping you plan worship using songs in *The Faith We Sing*. It is not intended to provide background material on each song, as a companion to a hymnal might do, although some articles may mention the background of a particular song. Instead, it offers practical tools and suggestions for use of these songs in worship.

The opening article by Hoyt L. Hickman, general editor of *The Faith We Sing*, addresses the history of this particular supplement, its various editions, suggestions for introducing the Supplement to your congregation, and the various styles of music included in it. He also discusses the nature of blended worship and the basic pattern of Christian worship. This article will be especially helpful for worship leaders who are new to contemporary worship music and blended styles of worship.

The commentaries on each hymn include the themes found within each song, appropriate places in worship to sing the songs, related scripture passages, creative use of the songs as acts of worship and with other acts of worship, recommended tempo markings, and suggestions for teaching the songs to your congregation. Some of these suggestions will work beautifully in your congregation. Others may not work in your particular setting. Use the commentaries as a starting point in your own prayerful planning of worship, allowing the creative Spirit to work within and through your planning process.

In addition to the commentaries, there are a number of indexes that will assist your worship planning. These indexes include many found in traditional hymnals, such as tune name index and metrical index. In addition, there is an index of suggested medleys, which includes companion songs and hymns in this Supplement, as well as hymns in *The United Methodist Hymnal*. The index of keys will help worship leaders who wish to plan their own medleys or who design the service to flow musically from one act of worship to the next.

The commentaries on each song were written by experts in various styles of worship music. Their knowledge about worship music is vast, and their suggestions have been tested by years of experience and the singing of many congregations. I am awed by their expertise, generous spirit, and desire to serve God through music. I am indebted to their contributions to this volume: David L. Bone, J. Michael Bryan, Jerry Carraway, Melva Costen, C. Michael Hawn, Hoyt L. Hickman, Lynn Hurst, Dan Landes, Raquel Mora Martínez, Dean McIntyre, Cathy Townley, Dwight Vogel , and Robin Knowles Wallace.

I am also deeply grateful to the other members of the editorial team of *The Faith We Sing* for the chance to work with them on such an exciting project: Hoyt L. Hickman, Gary Alan Smith, Daniel Benedict, Dean McIntyre, Bill Gnegy, Donna Nowels, Julianne Eriksen, and book design manager, Linda Bryant.

I pray that this volume will assist your worship planning and enable the people you serve to experience God's presence in powerful and life-changing ways through vital, creative, Spirit-filled worship.

Anne Burnette Hook, Worship Planner Editor

HOW TO USE *THE FAITH WE SING*

What Is *The Faith We Sing?*

The Faith We Sing is a response to the flood of new music that has been bringing new life to congregational singing. Even recent denominational hymnals, such as *The United Methodist Hymnal* (1989), need to be supplemented if congregations are to take advantage of this new music. Because the new music is coming from so many diverse sectors of the worldwide Christian community, there is a pressing need for a comprehensive supplemental hymnal that reflects this diversity. *The Faith We Sing* is an attempt to meet this need.

Current denominational hymnals also omit some older hymns and songs that continue to speak to the present generation. During the development of this Supplement, many of these were suggested, and a large number of them have been included. Adding these to the new music gives this collection a "something old, something new" character in harmony with the "blended worship" that meets the needs of many congregations today. Also, the compilers of this Supplement carefully considered what types and categories of music are underrepresented in current denominational hymnals, such as *The United Methodist Hymnal*, and are especially needed in any supplement.

This is a hymnal *supplement*, not a new hymnal. It makes no claim to be the only hymnal a congregation will need. It is designed to be used together with a standard hymnal and perhaps other resources as well. It was designed not to duplicate *The United Methodist Hymnal* in any way, and there is little duplication of other existing hymnals.

A Package of Resources

Hymnals and hymnal supplements today can no longer be single all-purpose books, along with an accompanist's edition. Musical styles are diverse, accompaniments have grown more complex and use a variety of instruments, and electronics is here to stay. For this reason, *The Faith We Sing* comes as a package of resources, including:

1. Pew Edition. This is the book from which the congregation sings, the basic book in the package. The most noticeable change from older hymnals is that for most of the music only the melody line is printed. This is done for music written to be sung in unison and never intended to be sung in harmony. The familiar format with four-part vocal harmony is still used for music written to be sung in harmony. There are occasional descants, echoes, and canons. This format has two advantages. First, it is more compact, allowing more music to be included without making the book too large and costly. Second, it is easier for persons in the congregation to read, omitting notations of interest only to accompanists. It also helps people pay more attention to the words and the meaning of what they are singing.

Another difference from most older hymnals is that instead of several indexes in the back there is only the Index of First Lines and Common Titles.

This is the only index persons in the congregation are likely to need, and it saves valuable space for more music. Other indexes, which only planners of worship need, are in the book you are reading.

Occasionally only the refrain of a song is printed, and the stanzas are in the Singer's Edition. This is done where the stanzas were written to be sung by a soloist or smaller ensemble, with the congregation joining in on the refrain.

2. Singer's Edition. This is designed for choirs, ensembles, and praise teams. It contains only vocal parts, with no accompaniments. Choral arrangements, where appropriate, are scored for various voicings, including two-, three-, and four-part harmony. There are also entire musical arrangements—including descants and optional endings. This edition also includes stanzas for songs intended to be sung by a soloist or smaller ensemble, where the Pew Edition contains only the refrain. Churches are encouraged to buy copies of this edition for the entire choir or praise team.

3. Accompaniment Edition. This is designed for the pianist, organist, and music leader. It features independent piano parts that support the melody and choral harmonies but in many cases do not duplicate them. It contains everything in the Singer's Edition and indicates the voicing contained in the Pew Edition. It includes full arrangements of each selection—introduction, modulations, and optional endings, where they exist.

If desired, music leaders can rehearse singers or even lead worship from the keyboard using either the keyboard accompaniment as written or the chord symbols as a guide. Bass guitar players can use the bass lines or chord symbols in this edition as their guide.

4. Simplified Edition. This is a moderately easy accompaniment edition with the melody as the top note in the right hand. It also includes descant lines where they exist, simplified guitar chords, and all lyrics. It can be used by persons with limited accompaniment skills.

It is well suited for use at home, church school, small group, and many other worship settings. In congregational worship it may be used simultaneously with other accompaniment and instrumental editions, since it follows the complete arrangements—including introductions, modulations, and optional endings.

5. Guitar Edition. This is designed for lead and rhythm guitar players. It can also be used by instrumentalists who play from lead sheets and by worship leaders who lead using a guitar. Note, however, that bass guitarists should use chord symbols or the bass lines in the Accompaniment Edition.

Each song contains the melody, lyrics, and grids of guitar chords used. Complicated chords have been simplified, yet the chords in this book still work with the chords in other editions. A complete chart of all guitar chords is included in the back of this edition.

6. MIDI Edition (electronic). This is designed for worship leaders who use MIDI-enabled keyboard instruments in worship. Each selection is orchestrated according to General MIDI specifications and presents the entire musical arrangement based on that in the Accompaniment Edition. This format offers the additional flexibility of using live instruments to play along as well as the ability to transpose, change tempo, or add or delete stanzas.

7. Compact Disc Accompaniment Edition (electronic). This set of compact discs, containing the complete contents of *The Faith We Sing*, is recorded from the above MIDI files. It enables pastors and other worship leaders to provide instrumental musical accompaniment when a pianist or organist is not available. It is also ideal for nursing homes, with shut-ins, at camps and retreats, and in many other settings outside the walls of the church building.

8. Worship Planner Edition. This is what you are reading now. It is designed for use by pastors, music leaders, worship planning teams, and all those who plan worship—in congregations, special meetings, church school, other organizations, and small groups. It contains material needed for the worship planning process, including numerous indexes.

9. Worship Planner CD-ROM Edition (electronic). This contains the complete contents of both the Worship Planner Edition and *The United Methodist Hymnal*. It helps pastors and musicians search for hymns and songs that fit the worship service. Searches can be focused and narrowed using search templates based on scripture, lectionary, meter, key, or topics. Once a song is selected, MIDI files play back one stanza so that the planner can check the mood of the song for worship.

Using *The Faith We Sing* in Your Congregation

A resource such as this should be carefully introduced to a congregation. In this process pastor(s), music leader(s), and choir(s) should work as a team in planning and carrying out this introduction.

A good place to start is with "old favorites" that many, if not most, of the congregation already know and love. Carefully look through *The Faith We Sing* and identify these. When in doubt, seek the advice of other persons who know the congregation well. Have the congregation begin using this Supplement by singing some of these favorites, either as part of regular weekly worship or in a hymn sing or songfest.

With music that is not already familiar to the people, a choir can be extremely helpful. They can carefully select and rehearse what is to be introduced to the congregation and sing it the first time as choir music. If there is anything "tricky" about the rhythm or the melody, they can practice to "get it right" and make it seem easy. A choir's evident love of a piece of music will go a long way toward selling it to the people. When the congregation is asked to sing it, the choir should have rehearsed it and be ready to give the people a good strong lead.

In selecting the unfamiliar music to be introduced, it is important to realize that some pieces of music will be easier than others for the congregation to learn. Some music will be new to the people but in a style with which they are already familiar and comfortable. For example, if a congregation is used to singing praise choruses, that will make it easier for them to learn another praise chorus. People worship most readily in their "heart language"—the musical style as well as verbal language with which they feel at home.

But people's hearts need to grow; they need to be "stretched." Sometimes a musical style that at first strikes a congregation as strange catches on and becomes an acquired taste. Songs from Africa, for instance, have caught on with many people and opened up to them a whole new dimension in their worship. It is especially important that accompanist(s) and choir carefully prepare for their role in introducing music when it is in a style new to the people.

There are, of course, limits to what a congregation can or should learn to sing. There will be music in this Supplement that a particular congregation and its leaders will find inappropriate, or too difficult, or not needed for their worship. But what is inappropriate for one congregation may be just right for another. A hymn that is too difficult for your congregation may make a good hymn anthem for your choir. What is not needed this year may be welcomed another year.

As you, the planner or leader of worship, examine *The Faith We Sing*, look at each hymn, song, chorus, or response. Evaluate each one from the perspective of your congregation. Make lists of (1) what your congregation already knows and is prepared to sing now; (2) what would be worth learning and easy for them to learn; and (3) what would take longer to learn but would be worth the effort. Enlist whatever help you need from other members of the congregation in this project. Use these lists in your future worship planning.

After the congregation has first sung something, evaluate how well they have sung it. The teaching process will probably need to continue through well-planned repetition, especially if the music is not easy for them to learn. This may involve simply singing it again once or twice again that month. Or it may involve more work by the accompanist(s) or choir to help the congregation "get it right." Notes in the bulletin or newsletter or comments from the pulpit on its background and significance are often helpful. After the first month, use it again on appropriate occasions so that the congregation doesn't forget it.

The Challenge of Blended Worship

What is "blended worship," and why does it meet the needs of so many congregations today? Music is a cultural battleground in our society today. The kinds of music used in worship can be crucial in determining who feels welcome—and who does not—in a congregation. Generation and age level, culture and class, race and ethnicity are important in where one feels at home. These are all reflected in the diversity of music played in churches today. There are often conflicts in tastes between the people who now worship in a congregation and those in the surrounding community whom that congregation wishes to attract. Within a congregation there is often a conflict of tastes between generations or other factions.

Worship, and especially music, are often described as polarized between traditional and contemporary; but it is not that simple. There are many kinds of traditional and many kinds of contemporary. What a congregation regards as traditional depends on what it has grown accustomed to. Anything that has been done for very long has become "traditional." What is considered "contemporary" depends upon which voices in our diverse contemporary world one is listening to.

No one congregation can reach everyone. There is a God-given "diversity of gifts." A congregation and its leaders need to discern the particular ministries for which they are gifted and to which they are called. They need to know their community well enough to discern where its needs and the congregation's actual or potential gifts overlap.

A congregation that is able to have two or more services each week can extend its ministries if each weekly service has its own distinctive style, but for many congregations this is not feasible. There may not be enough people, money, and gifted and trained leadership. The danger may be too great that separately worshiping factions would drift farther and farther apart.

Even a congregation—or weekly service—clearly ministering to a certain segment of the community is likely to find that segment divided in its tastes. Musical tastes often divide parents from children, husbands from wives, friends from friends. They divide people of the same generation, race, ethnicity, or class.

Moreover, many persons prefer blended worship. Their tastes are wideranging. They enjoy being "stretched" and know it is good for them. They want to identify with the whole diverse and universal church—"the communion of saints." So, by necessity or by choice, a great many congregations find themselves with a service in which people of diverse tastes meet for worship. For such services this Supplement will prove a rich resource. In it is a wide variety of music for congregational singing in several major categories.

1. Hymns, old and new. If you missed an old favorite in your current hymnal, it just might be in this Supplement. If you doubt that great hymns are still being written, look and sing through this Supplement.

2. Gospel songs. The Supplement includes not only contemporary gospel but also traditional gospel songs you may have learned and loved from a book such as *The Cokesbury Worship Hymnal*.

3. Contemporary praise choruses. Praise choruses that have swept the country in recent years and older choruses, such as "Into My Heart" (2160), are featured.

4. American ethnic music. African American songs from spirituals to contemporary are featured. Hispanic/Latino songs are also included.

5. Global music. Songs from Africa, Asia, Latin America, and Europe are featured in the Supplement, as well as music gathered from around the world by the Iona Community in Scotland.

6. Taizé music. This music is a powerfully emotional, haunting form of chanting that has spread from the Taizé community in France and has been taken up by many Americans. Some congregations have found that services in this style can reach a kind of seeker that churches have otherwise been unable to reach.

Because Taizé music is so unique, more needs to be said about its origins and performance style. Taizé is an ecumenical monastic community in France.

Each year it attracts young people from all over the world seeking to experi-ence God through the community's unique style of worship and praise. Taizé music is sung in a very particular way, due to the intent of the brothers who created this unique form of worship song. The brothers wanted worship songs that everyone could actively participate in, not just listen to. The global nature of their worshiping community led them to create short, repetitive songs in a variety of languages that can be easily learned by rote.

Singing Taizé music is simple. A song is started by the song leader. The members of the congregation join in as the song is repeated and they feel com-fortable. Various instruments are added and taken away. The song ends accord-ing to the leading of the Spirit, dying as the congregation moves into prayer.

The Taizé songs in this Supplement may certainly be sung in this way. However, they may also be used in a more traditional manner, singing them once or twice as an act of worship. For more information and resources about Taizé music, contact GIA Publications, Chicago, Illinois—the U.S. distributor for Taizé music and worship materials.

7. Service music and responses. If you think you couldn't be interested in this category, look at 2275.

Patterns of Worship

There are two worship patterns that are basic to your planning the week-by-week use of this Supplement as well as your basic hymnal and other resources.

1. The first of these is the calendar—your actual week-by-week schedule of services and service texts or themes. This includes whatever days and seasons of the traditional and ecumenical Christian Year you observe and also other special days and occasions in the year that you observe by local or civic custom. This Supplement includes additional music for the great days and seasons of the Christian Year. Also, the Supplement committee was asked to include a good Mother's Day hymn, so we have included "A Mother Lined a Basket" (2189). The most requested hymn in this Supplement is "Eternal Father, Strong to Save" (2191), which is both a hymn for safety at sea and is also known as The Navy Hymn.

However you plan your congregation's services, it is essential over time to cover the whole basic Christian story and teachings. We believe that with a standard hymnal and this Supplement it should be possible to select hymns and songs that cover this whole range.

2. The second is the pattern of each service, into which each hymn or song is fitted. Diverse as these patterns are from congregation to congregation and from service to service, there is a basic pattern that underlies most congregational worship. It is important to be sensitive to this basic pattern in selecting music. This pattern is based on the belief that Christian public worship is an encounter with the living God through the risen Christ in the power of the Holy Spirit. The Emmaus account in Luke 24:13-35 is a model for worship today. We might call the four components of this basic pattern (1) Entrance; (2) Proclamation and Response; (3) Thanksgiving and Communion; and (4) Sending Forth.

1. Entrance

The risen Christ joined two disciples as they walked together on the road to Emmaus. Likewise, in the power of the Holy Spirit, the risen and ascended Christ joins us when we gather for worship.

Christian public worship, like all human assemblies, begins with gathering and opening exchanges. We, however, gather *in the Lord's name*. Our exchanges are not only with one another but also with the living God, who comes to us through the risen Christ. The "we" who gather includes not only those visibly present but also, invisibly, the whole "communion of saints"—the universal church of all times and all places. Some of us, unlike the disciples on the Emmaus road, come expecting an encounter with God. Others, like those disciples, are not.

Those disciples poured out their sorrow to the Christ they did not recognize and in so doing opened their hearts to what was about to happen. Likewise, we pour out whatever is on our hearts and thereby open ourselves to the Word that is to follow.

Singing has a crucial place in this pouring out of our hearts. It incomparably deepens the expression of our feelings and opens us to what God has to share with us. Often this part of the service is mainly sung.

Since the community gathers in faith, this first part of the service is likely to be mainly praise and prayer. It may begin with a spoken or sung call to praise and worship. The praise itself can take many forms, most of which involve singing. It may, for instance, consist of a single opening hymn or song of praise, or a medley of praise choruses, or an extended praise service. There may or may not be a processional involving clergy, choir(s), and others—sometimes even the whole congregation. There may be introit, anthem(s), solo(s). Praise can range from awed adoration to joyous thanksgiving. Prayer may be spoken or sung and extends beyond praise. It may, for example, be invocation, confession, or petition. On a day like Ash Wednesday, or on an occasion where the congregation has been stunned by an overwhelming tragedy, praise may be slow in coming and other forms of prayer predominate during the Entrance. The Supplement includes hymns that are specifically tailored for the opening of worship (2270-2274), and a large portion of the rest of the music is equally suitable for opening praise and prayer.

The Entrance is not limited to praise and prayer. Acts of centering that are not, strictly speaking, praise or prayer may fill a need. Some congregations sing a centering hymn or song such as "Come and Find the Quiet Center" (2128) or "Blessed Quietness" (2142). A service targeted to seekers who are not immediately ready for praise and prayer may substitute other acts (including music) that speak to the seeker's condition.

But in all this diversity there is a basic unity of purpose to the Entrance. It is to open and prepare us for the proclamation of the Word that is to follow. It encourages and enables us to move from whatever states of mind and spirit we are in when we gather to a state of readiness and receptivity when the Word is proclaimed. It is to build and strengthen community among the worshipers and clear the channels for communion with God. It is *entrance* into focused awareness of the presence of the living God and into an attentive listening for God's Word.

In building and strengthening community among the worshipers we include those invisibly, as well as visibly, present—"the communion of saints." This is one reason for a congregation's musical tastes to be "stretched." The "something new, something old" of blended worship gives expression to our ancestors in the faith as they invisibly join those who have contemporary tastes. Singing music from many nations and ethnic communities, and in languages other than our own, reminds us that we are being joined in worship by "a great multitude that no one could count, from every nation, from all tribes and peoples and languages" (Rev. 7:9). The church of "all times and all places" deserves to sit at our worship planning table. This Supplement is a reminder of that fact.

Another question arises as we move from Entrance toward Proclamation and Response. Should every service be planned from beginning to end around a particular theme? Should the Entrance also center around that theme? That depends. It makes sense for a service to have a "plot" that prepares for that day's proclamation of the Word, then "preaches for a verdict," and then looks for an appropriate response. Sometimes the people come expectant and ready for the theme of the day. One may surely sing Christmas carols from beginning to end on Christmas Eve and sing Easter music throughout the service on Easter Day.

On most days, however, the congregation has little idea what the theme of the proclamation will be until the proclamation begins. Allusions to the theme in a hymn or song earlier in the service are not likely to be noticed.

Furthermore, persons come to worship with very diverse needs and hopes, and the theme of the day may not be relevant to everyone's condition. Many have gone out from a service not particularly helped by the sermon, but richly blessed by the praise, the prayer, or by Holy Communion. There are reasons why nonthematic hymns of praise and praise choruses are usually so prominent in worship—and in this Supplement. In themselves, they bring a rich variety of blessings to persons with diverse needs. Also, by relating persons to God they effectively open up channels for their hearing of God's Word—whatever the theme of the day.

2. Proclamation and Response

When the disciples on the Emmaus road had poured out their hearts to the risen Christ, he "opened the scriptures" to them and "interpreted to them the things about himself in all the scriptures" (Luke 24:27). They later told how their hearts had burned within them as he did this.

Today the scriptures are opened to the people through such means as scripture readings, preaching, witnessing, music (such as a cantata or a musical), and other arts and media (such as video or live drama). The purpose is to let scripture speak in all its power so that the people may find in it God's Word.

These acts of proclamation are frequently interspersed with responses in a call and response pattern. We listen for the Word of God speaking to us through these acts. As we hear something that speaks to our condition, our hearts may burn as surely as hearts burned on the Emmaus road. Singing a psalm, an anthem, a hymn, or a song gives opportunity for the burning of our hearts to find expression.

A hymn or song in this part of the service tends to be thematic. It is a response to what has immediately preceded it (such as a scripture reading) and a preparation for what immediately follows (such as the sermon). As such, it should be carefully selected so as to express and advance what is being proclaimed.

On the other hand, one need not feel frustrated if no hymn or song exactly fits the message. A prayer hymn for illumination such as "Break Thou the Bread of Life" (in most standard hymnals) can appropriately precede any proclamation of the Word. A hymn, song, or chorus of praise is a fitting response to a scripture reading. A hymn of invitation to Christian discipleship or of Christian commitment need not be thematic to be a fitting response to preaching.

This Supplement, however, contains some excellent hymns and songs for baptism, confirmation, and other acts of Christian commitment. Selections from 2247 to 2253 relate specifically to baptism, and "At the Font We Start Our Journey" (2114) relates to baptism at Easter. "I Was There to Hear Your Borning Cry" (2051) has become a popular hymn for baptisms, confirmations, and other crucial points in the life cycle. Hymns and songs relating specifically to Christian commitment comprise much of the whole central part of the Supplement.

There are many choruses, responses, and acclamations that can come at almost any point in the service. For instance, the three alleluias in the supplement (2014, 2043, and 2078) and the alleluias in standard hymnals can be sung, as is traditional, before the Gospel reading to greet the risen Christ whose words we are about to hear. But alleluias are appropriate at other points in the service as well. And in some congregations an announcement of joyous news is likely to bring forth spontaneous alleluias—prompted by the leader or by someone in the congregation—sung to a tune the congregation knows.

Likewise, there is a rich selection in the Supplement from which a call to prayer or prayer response could be selected, as well as a popular setting of the Lord's Prayer (2278).

3. Holy Communion

When the two disciples and the risen Christ reached Emmaus they sat down at table to eat together. Likewise, we join at the Lord's Table with the risen Christ in the holy meal known variously as Holy Communion, Lord's Supper, or Eucharist.

Jesus took, blessed, broke, and gave the bread, just as he had done three days earlier in the upper room, and earlier when he had fed the hungry multitudes. Now, in the name of the risen Christ, we do these same four actions with the bread and cup. As he was "made known to them in the breaking of the bread," so the risen and ascended Christ can be known to us as we commune with him.

In the Supplement, many communion hymns are added to those now in standard hymnals (2254-2269). Communion hymns may be sung before Holy Communion, during the giving of the bread and cup, and after communion. Other hymns in the Supplement, such as "All Who Hunger" (2126), are also good communion hymns.

In services where persons leave their seats and go forward to receive communion it helps those who are away from their seats to participate in the singing if the hymn, song, or chorus is familiar to the people, or if the words are shown on large screens.

A full musical setting of Holy Communion (Sursum Corda, Sanctus and Benedictus, Memorial Acclamation, and Great Amen) by contemporary composer Mark A. Miller is also provided in the Supplement (2257). Those who also wish to sing a Kyrie and a Gloria in Excelsis earlier in the service will find new settings of them as well (2127, 2275-2277).

4. Sending Forth

Jesus disappeared so as to send those disciples out into the world to share their faith and joy with others. Likewise, he sends us forth into the world.

While a closing hymn may be one of Christian commitment (see above), it is often a hymn of sending forth. It may be a recessional. We go out singing. The Supplement provides hymns specifically for sending forth (2279-2281).

When those ancient disciples arrived at Jerusalem later that evening, they found Christ again. Today, we can find Christ with us wherever we go.

May your use of *The Faith We Sing* help those for whom you plan so to worship—and so to go out from worship—that the living God may be with you through the risen Christ in the power of the Holy Spirit.

Hoyt L. Hickman, General Editor

Editor's Note: For additional information, visit cokesburymusic.com.

COMMENTARY ON HYMNS

A Hymn for Deacons (2245)
See "Within the day-to-day."

A mother lined a basket (2189)
Themes: Mother's Day; children; graduation

This effective hymn is a wonderful addition for churches that may shy away from Mother's Day. The fourth stanza also makes it a great selection for a graduation ceremony. However, be prepared: the fourth stanza can have a surprising emotional impact because of its directness.

The Singer's Edition contains parts that let the choir take an active role in introducing the hymn. Use the choral harmonization on stanza 3, then invite the congregation to join on stanza 4, adding the descant as well. A simple approach will also work with three soloists singing stanzas 1-3, and the congregation singing stanza 4. A cello or flute playing the melody as an introduction would be nice. Accompany with organ playing all the notes of the accompaniment except the melody.

Advent Song (2090)
See "Light the Advent candle."

African Processional (2035)
See "Praise, praise, praise the Lord."

All hail King Jesus (2069)
Themes: Adoration and praise of Jesus; life everlasting

Palm Sunday and Christ the King Sunday are two very appropriate times for this majestic praise song, although it can be used anytime of the year. It works well as the opening song for a service with a theme on the majesty and glory of Jesus. A nice opening musical sequence would be "All Hail King Jesus" followed by a modulation into "O Worship the King" (UMH, 73). If using a praise band, keep the four-part hymn style as majestic as possible. Other songs that work well with it are "Hosanna! Hosanna!" (2109), "He Is Exalted" (2070), and "We Will Glorify the King of Kings" (2087).

All I need is you (2080)

Themes: Grace; God's provision; hope

This simple song recognizes God in Christ as the source of all we need, want, and hope for. It could be appropriately sung before or after prayers of petition, or as a call to prayer or response to prayer. It could also function as a sung response after a psalm of God's provision, such as Psalm 23 (UMH, 754).

Piano could accompany this song alone, or quietly played guitar, electronic keyboard, and/or organ could be effective. In any case, the accompaniment should be simple, so as not to overshadow the lyrics.

All the gifts that God has given (2240)

Themes: The fellowship of believers; service; diversity

With a text based on Ephesians 4:6-7, "One God and Father of Us All" calls the fellowship of believers to unity through their diversity. A beautiful way to introduce this song would be to use a tapestry. Show the back of the tapestry first—usually not a beautiful sight. Point out the different colors, the lack of pattern, the knots, and the seemingly haphazard organization. Then, show the front side. Point out how the Master Designer can take people from all imaginable backgrounds and cultures, people with different gifts and talents, and weave them into something beautiful.

Introduce the chorus and then invite the congregation to sing it again. A soloist continues by singing the verses and the congregation joins in on the chorus.

All who hunger (2126)

Themes: Gathering for worship; Holy Communion

This hymn affirms that Holy Communion is a uniting of all the people of God, despite their wandering, searching, restlessness, loneliness, and longing, into one family gathered around the table to taste and see the goodness of God. It affords the opportunity for men to sing one stanza, women another, and to join on the third. Other options include having only the melody sung by women on stanza 1, with altos adding harmony on stanza 2, and men with all parts on the last stanza. Yet a third possibility comes from the simplicity of the bass line, which contains only two different notes—G and D. Have a song leader rehearse the men's voices in singing the true bass line, indicating the tonic G with a lower hand position than the dominant D. Then have men sing stanza 1 using only those two pitches (*a cappella*), with women joining only on the melody for stanza 2, and all parts plus accompaniment on the last stanza.

In ordinary congregational singing of this hymn, organists might lend a quality of tension and release by sustaining a dominant D pedal at the start of stanza 2, resolving into the tonic G only on the final note.

This tune lends itself to singing in canon (in a round). Start a new section on the beginning of each measure (or every two beats, if you are ambitious!). When singing in this manner, eliminate accompaniment. The third verse should be sung in unison ("All who hunger, sing *together*"). An alternate choral harmonization is included in the Accompaniment and Singer's Editions.

Alleluia (Celtic) (2043)
Themes: Praise; thanksgiving; gratitude

Sing this simple, folklike alleluia unaccompanied or reinforce it with flute and guitar. A light hand drum might support the rhythm when sung unaccompanied. The lilting, dancelike quality of the melody has its own charm without adding too many additional sounds.

This selection makes an excellent response to the Gospel lesson or a psalm response to appropriate psalms of praise, such as Psalm 100 and 150. It may also serve as a preparation for or a response to prayers of thanksgiving or praise within the service.

Alleluia (Honduras) (2078)
Themes: Praise; thanksgiving; resurrection; Easter

This alleluia from Honduras is ideal for a response to the Gospel lesson on Easter Sunday. Because the risen Christ is the major theme of all Christian worship, it can be used on any Sunday, however. It would serve as an excellent processional for the choir as well. Another possibility would be to continue the long-standing practice of Christianizing the psalms by using this song as a response to the psalm for Easter—Psalm 118. It would make an excellent selection to sing during communion as the congregation receives the elements.

Start it gently and let it build through the singing. It can be sung unaccompanied or with a simple guitar strum and various rhythm instruments. Three verses are included in the Accompaniment Edition. Have a soloist sing these verses. Singing the refrain in Spanish is quite easy and would be a significant gesture of hospitality to those in your congregation for whom Spanish is their first language.

Alleluia (Taizé) (2014)
Themes: Praise; thanksgiving; gratitude

This is one of the most familiar alleluia responses used by the Taizé Community, an ecumenical monastic order in France. It is instantly accessible to all gathered. Sing it in a lively and energetic manner.

This song may be used in several ways. It is effective as a response following the Gospel lesson or as a psalm response for appropriate psalms of thanksgiving, such as Psalms 96, 98, 100, 117, and 150. As a response to prayers of thanksgiving and praise, a congregation might sing the refrain twice in preparation for the prayers. As each expression of thanksgiving is given, sing only the second line as a short response. An instrumental accompaniment supports the music, such as guitar, oboe, cello, or even trumpet. It is also effective when sung unaccompanied.

Amen, Amen (2072)
Theme: The life of Christ

Amen! Thus, it is written, and so it is true! This response is repeated over and over again as the song leader as storyteller narrates the familiar story of Jesus the Christ from birth to death. The story takes on increased energy after the third verse as the creative instrumentalist modulates one-half step for stanzas 4 (F#), 5 (G), and 6 (G# to enharmonic A♭).

In keeping with other songs in which the congregation is prone to accompany the sung word with rhythmic clapping, care should be taken to avoid overshadowing the message with the accompaniment.

Amen Siakudumisa (2067)

See "Amen, we praise your name, O God."

Amen, we praise your name, O God (2067)
Amen Siakudumisa
Themes: Praise; thanksgiving; gratitude

This song was written by Roman Catholic musician S. C. Molefe during a group composition session conducted by ethnomusicologist David Dargie. It was designed to be used at the conclusion of the Great Thanksgiving or communion prayer, where the congregation voices an "Amen." Xhosa Methodist congregations in South Africa often sing it as a response for the Te Deum ("We praise you, O God"), a common feature of worship there. This song may be sung as a choir processional and as a response to any psalm of praise and thanksgiving as well.

It is to be sung with energy and a steady beat. Xhosa traditional music does not use drums. This music is usually sung unaccompanied. Movement or swaying is always appropriate when singing African music. The congregation might enjoy swaying to the beat in the following manner: small step right, close with left foot; small step left, close with right foot. This step would take two complete measures. In much African music it is important to have singing across a sustained section at the end of a phrase. Notice that the bass part and the leader's part accomplish this. Sing several times until the song builds dynamically and in intensity. The congregation can learn the African dialect almost immediately and will enjoy singing it. Do not slow the tempo once the music starts. Keep it steady right to the end of the singing and dancing.

An outcast among outcasts (2104)
Themes: Thanksgiving; Jesus' death and Resurrection; justice

Two events from Jesus' life (the healing of the ten lepers and the Crucifixion) are recalled in this hymn. These stories remind us that God's power comes first to those with little worldly power or status. This hymn is appropriate anytime the sermon or worship theme focuses on our call to be with those who are poor and powerless in our society. Stanzas 1 and 3 might be combined with the Luke reading for a Thanksgiving service. Stanzas 2 and 3 might be appropriate on the Sundays immediately following Easter.

This hymn tune is somewhat familiar. Keyboard accompaniment is best. Stanza 1 may be accompanied and sung quietly. Build intensity especially toward the end of stanza 2, and sing stanza 3 with a sense of great triumph. The alternate organ harmonization in the Accompaniment Edition is very appropriate for stanza 3.

Arise, shine (2005)
Themes: The completion of Creation; the city of God; the glory of God; Epiphany

"Arise, Shine" is a refreshing call and response version of the text from Isaiah 60. Traditionally known as one of the lesser canticles from the Old Testament, this chorus could be effectively used during the season of Epiphany when there may be an emphasis on the completion of God's Creation. The choir or a soloist could serve as the leader with the congregation responding. Since the text is simple and easy to memorize, the congregation could learn this chorus with little or no rehearsal.

Use this song with the written accompaniment or sing it with no accompaniment. The inclusion of chord symbols will be helpful for improvisation on multiple repetitions. If a guitar accompaniment is used, the fast-changing harmonic rhythm may prove to be impractical. Try playing only the chords written on beats 1 and 4.

As a fire is meant for burning (2237)
Themes: Mission; witness; discipleship; hope

Using 2 Corinthians 4:7 and Matthew 4:14-16, Ruth Duck's text paraphrases and develops Emil Brunner's observation that just as a fire is meant for burning, so the church is meant for loving. This hymn may be especially appropriate in spring (note the reference to the "green bud" in stanza 3) or on the Sundays after Pentecost (when the flame image and the focus on the church's mission are especially relevant).

The tune BEACH SPRING will be familiar to many congregations. It may be introduced by having a recorder or flute play the melody line. This tune is from the Sacred Harp tradition; because Sacred Harp singing is unaccompanied, congregations who can do part singing *a cappella* will find that an effective approach. If accompaniment is used, it should be light rather than heavy, not calling attention to itself.

As the deer (2025)
Themes: Aspiration; commitment

This beautiful song by Martin J. Nystrom flowed from his heart while he was meditating on Psalm 42. It remains one of the most popular songs from the new contemporary music genre.

Its slow ($\quarternote$ = 72-80), meditative style fits well during a time of contemplation, when the worshiper is asked to reflect on how he or she will respond to God. It is also appropriate before a time of prayer or the spoken word. A medley of worship songs might include "Open Our Eyes" (2086), "As the Deer" (2025), and "O Lord, You're Beautiful" (2064). The stanza should be sung in unison; while the refrain ("You alone are my strength, my shield") should be sung in parts. Although only one stanza is published here, two other stanzas can be found in other publications. This song should depict a simple reverence in its style.

As we gather at your table (2268)
Themes: Holy Communion; sending forth

This hymn is especially appropriate as a conclusion to the sacrament, or as a final hymn of benediction and sending forth. As a sending forth, it is not a triumphant conclusion to worship. Instead, it sends the congregation forth with the call to witness to the world of our love for Christ by living life as if it were a sacramental act. It is we, in the name of Christ, who bring peace, compassion, and salvation.

Chávez-Melo's music for this hymn has a haunting, expressive quality. An oboe or a cello can impart this quality to the congregation as an introduction. The leaps in the melody, though not particularly difficult, are unexpected and more frequent than those in many other hymn melodies, and the keyboard accompanist should play the melody prominently.

At the font we start our journey (2114)
Theme: Christian life and journey

This hymn uses four specific locations important in worship in order to illustrate the claim and call upon our lives as believers in the resurrected Christ. The hymn is unified through its centering on Easter—baptism of believers, our becoming witnesses to the Resurrection through its retelling, continued nourishing through communion, and commissioning as ministers to the world as we leave through the sanctuary doors. This unity through the Easter theme, as well as the majestic LAUDA ANIMA tune, makes it a fine Easter hymn.

The unique quality of the individual stanzas, however, as each comments upon font, pulpit, altar, and door, provides opportunity to use each stanza before or after baptism, sermon, communion, and sending forth, either as a congregational or choir response. The text might also be used to teach young Sunday school classes, confirmation classes, or Christian initiation sessions about the hows and whys of worship.

Awesome God **(2040)**
See "Our God is an awesome God."

Baptized in water (2248)

Themes: Baptism; renewal of the baptismal covenant; confirmation

This text celebrates the key theme of the baptismal covenant: "born of water and the Spirit." Especially appropriate when persons are anointed with the sign of the cross on their foreheads (whether in connection with baptism, confirmation, baptismal renewal, or Christian initiation), this text lifts up the primary symbols of the baptismal covenant.

Congregations who sing "Morning Has Broken" will be familiar with the tune. An alternate wording for the last half of the last stanza would be: "Born to one fam-'ly, sisters and brothers, joyfully now God's praises we sing."

Be still and know (2057)

Themes: Assurance; presence of God; providence of God; hope

This is one of many shorter ("wee") songs of the Iona Community in Scotland. It is most effective when sung unaccompanied. A single voice can introduce the song and all gathered will be able to repeat it quickly. A solo flute or oboe could also introduce the melody before the soloist begins.

Use as a psalm response to Psalm 46, from which it is taken (v. 10), or as a preparation for morning prayer. Sing it in unison before the prayer at least twice. At the conclusion of the prayer sing it again, this time in canon. The second part may be reinforced by the flute or oboe. The canon may be indicated by dividing the congregation into two parts with a simple gesture or by inviting men to begin and women to follow. The choir may also sing the second part of the canon after the congregation begins. Children may introduce this song to the congregation very effectively.

Bind us together (2226)

Themes: Fellowship; unity; community; the church

This chorus is especially appropriate when the scriptures in worship focus on the theme of unity, such as Psalm 133; Ecclesiastes 4:9-12; John 17:20-21; or Ephesians 4:3-6. Accompanied by an acoustic guitar, this simple chorus calls for unity in the Body of Christ. Have your liturgical dance troupe interpret this song as a soloist sings; then, invite the congregation to make this their prayer as it is sung together. Many congregations have also used this song as a benediction at the close of evening vespers or prayer. It should be sung quietly and reflectively as a prayer unto God. Optional choral parts are included in the Accompaniment and Singer's Editions.

Bless His Holy Name (2015)
See "Bless the Lord, O my soul."

Bless the Lord my soul (Taizé) (2013)
Themes: Thanksgiving; praise; gratitude
This is one of the most familiar and often used shorter songs from the Taizé Community, an ecumenical monastic order in France. The four simple phrases (ABAC form) make it easy to sing without music after just a few repetitions. This style of music is often used as a centering prayer. In the Taizé Community, the assembly soon lose themselves in the singing experience. The song supports personal prayer and meditation.

As a meditative selection, sing "Bless the Lord" in preparation for or in response to prayers of thanksgiving. Use this song as a response for Psalm 103, from which the opening phrase is taken. Sing unaccompanied or with a few supportive instruments. In the Accompaniment Edition, parts are provided for various instruments and for a song leader to sing above the congregation's version. These parts add variety as the song is repeated and helps maintain energy during the repetitions. "Bless the Lord" may also be sung during communion. Repeat at least three times when used for facilitating centering or meditation.

Bless the Lord, O my soul (2015)
Themes: Praise; thanksgiving; gratitude
This chorus, which is based on Psalm 103, works well as a call and response. Use a vocal team or choir to lead the congregation into an affirmation of faith, or a time of prayer and singing. Have a solo voice sing the opening phrases and have the congregation repeat them. In the middle section ("He has done great things"), have the congregation repeat these phrases after the song leader in the same manner as the first section. Everyone sings the last section together.

When used as a call to prayer, have the accompanist play the middle section as someone reads a short verse or psalm, or ask people to spend a few moments in meditation thinking of those things for which they are most thankful in their lives. Ask them to think how God is speaking to them. As a response to prayer, sing the middle section as a joyful affirmation of God's gracious works.

Blessed be the name of the Lord (2034)
Themes: Adoration and praise; the name of God; protection and refuge; strength
This high energy chorus, made popular by Carol Cymbala and the Brooklyn Tabernacle Choir, is a joyous, celebratory proclamation of Proverbs 18:10. The driving rhythm calls for percussion, whether it be a full trap set, conga drums or just the congregation praising the Lord with their hands on beats 2 and 4. After

you have sung the song through two or three times, have all of the instruments except the percussion drop out and sing the chorus *a cappella;* then, let the band rejoin the congregation for a final chorus. Suggestions are made for changing the words of the chorus each time it is sung to emphasize different characteristics of the name of the Lord. Feel free to make additional changes.

Blessed quietness (2142)
See "Joys are flowing like a river."

Blest are they (2155)
Themes: Jesus' life; the Beatitudes; peace; mercy; justice

This is a very moving and popular setting of the Beatitudes. It is appropriate anytime this passage appears in the lectionary or is used in worship. It would also be nice on Reign of Christ/Christ the King Sunday (the Sunday before Advent begins) or for an All Saints Day celebration.

Unless the congregation is very familiar with this song, ask them to sing the refrain only. Use soloists and small groups on the stanzas. The pitch range of these stanzas make them accessible to many teenage singers. Accompany on piano, guitar, and/or bass. Add the men's voice to the refrain after the third or fourth stanzas. Save the refrain descant until after the fifth stanza and repeat the refrain for a joyous close. You might experiment with adding treble voices to the men's part or male voices to the descant in these final refrains (in their own octave). Encourage improvisation from the singers. Make it a "glad" and joyous song! Simple movement (for choir or congregation) during the refrain is also a nice addition.

Bring Forth the Kingdom (2190)
See "You are salt for the earth."

Bring many names (2047)
Themes: God; justice; Creation; family

This hymn reminds us that God cannot be fully named by any one name. It would be appropriate on Trinity Sunday, which is also Peace with Justice Sunday in The United Methodist Church. On Mother's Day, stanzas 1 and 2 would be especially appropriate. On Father's Day, stanzas 1 and 3 would enhance worship.

The use of soloists can bring this hymn to life. The choir sings stanza 1, four soloists sing stanzas 2-5, and then choir and congregation sing stanza 6. The four soloists might join together in singing the stanza 6 descant. Embrace the challenge of the text by assigning soloists against type. Have a male sing about the "strong mother God." Ask a young child to sing about the "old aching God."

The hymn should flow in two beats per measure ($\downarrow$ = 60). The final stanza can be slower, with a more expansive tempo. The hymn may be approached in a traditional manner, but it can find expression when sung in a Broadway ballad style as well.

Broken for Me (2263)
Theme: Holy Communion

This simple, yet beautiful chorus would be appropriate anytime the sacrament of the Lord's Supper is observed, particularly during a Maundy Thursday service. The refrain is very simple and could be introduced to the congregation by a flute. Have a soloist sing the refrain once and then invite the congregation to join. The verses could be sung by a soloist or perhaps a children's choir, with the congregation singing the refrain after each verse. Alternate the verses between the soloist or choir and the instrumentalist, or have the instrumentalist play along with the soloist a third below the melody. This chorus would also be very effective with just guitar accompaniment.

Brother, sister, let me serve you (2222)
Themes: Friendship; bearing one another's burdens; community

What constitutes the Christian community is its unity of faith in the risen Lord, and its sharing with one another and the world in the love of Christ. This simple hymn proclaims that unity as it is expressed in the caring for one another, the bearing of one another's burdens, and the nurturing of one another in times of both need and joy.

The directness of the text will have special appeal to children, and this hymn would make a fine children's choir anthem. "The Servant Song" is especially suitable for Pentecost, or any other occasion when the theme focuses on what it means to be the church of Jesus Christ.

The first measure of the second phrase of each stanza contains some leaps and unexpected pitches that might be troublesome in learning this hymn. The four pitches of this measure should be rehearsed until secure. Then connect the phrase with the rather awkward approach from the end of the previous measure.

By the Babylonian rivers (2217)
Themes: Oppression; captivity

This short psalm of lament is a quiet prayer to God for deliverance. In its original context, that deliverance was from oppression at the hands of Israel's Babylonian captors. But in a symbolic sense, this hymn can be sung as a plea for deliverance from a number of forces that oppress people today: poverty, war, disease, drugs, physical abuse, racism, as well as political oppression.

The minor tonality, the seriousness and suffering in the text, and the repeatedly descending direction of the melodic line call for a quiet and reflective style of singing and accompaniment. A harp would make a fine accompanying instrument, especially if the melody is played or doubled by a soft flute or recorder. Other suitable accompanying instruments would include the acoustic guitar or an autoharp. Perhaps the organ can duplicate one of these instruments.

The first half of the first stanza can also be used as a sung response to a chanted or read psalm text.

Caminando (2235)
See "We are marching in the light of God."

Canto de Esperanza (2186)
See "May the God of hope go with us."

Cares Chorus (2215)
See "I cast all my cares upon you."

Carol of the Epiphany (2094)
See "I sought him dressed in finest clothes."

Celebrate love (2073)
Themes: Love; community

This is a good song to open a praise medley or to sing as an opening song. Its Caribbean rhythm and style suggest adding various rhythm instruments, such as a guiro (a fish-shaped scraping instrument), shaker, congas, and/or tambourine. Teach the congregation the refrain and have a soloist or the choir sing the verses. Because its melody is simple, this song is very effectively led by children. You also might teach the children simple hand motions or sign language to interpret parts of the song.

Consider having someone read a scripture passage, such as 2 Corinthians 5:17, after the refrain and before the verses of the song, as the music plays in the background. Repeat the refrain at the end several times, using only rhythm instruments to accompany on the last time.

"Celebrate Love" would also make a great congregational song for a wedding ceremony. Suggested tempo for the song is lively ($\quarternote$ = 120). Don't be afraid to clap!

Change my heart, O God (2152)
Themes: Grace; redemption; repentance; new birth; integrity; obedience to God

The lyrics in this song express a longing to be made new. It is appropriate as an act of repentance for believers. It would also work well in a communion service, perhaps just before the prayer of confession. To make it more corporate, try making the pronouns plural: "Change *our* hearts, O God."

Although acoustic guitar accompaniment is lovely on this song, piano or electronic keyboard set to either an electric piano sound or a combination of piano and strings would also work well. Depending on the pace of the service, a tempo from 72 to 86 beats per minute would be effective.

Child of promise (2249)
Theme: Baptism of infants or young children

Some congregations will be familiar with this song because of its inclusion in *The United Methodist Book of Worship.* Calling the one who is being baptized by name in the refrain is an unforgettable experience. The refrain of this song may be sung after each child is presented for baptism, and/or the entire song sung after the baptism when the congregation is introduced to their new brother or sister. When the baby cries, tradition says they will grow up to sing in the choir! In any event, the acceptance of crying as a part of a baby's life is part of a congregation's response (see stanza 4). The use of the name rather than the more generic "Child of promise" is strongly encouraged in most circumstances.

The tune is in the style of a children's lullaby. Accompaniment should be simple, direct, and uncomplicated. A quiet solo stop on the organ will be effective.

Christ beside me (2166)
Themes: The Christian life; courage; faith; grace; facing adversity

This hymn (also known as *St. Patrick's Breastplate,* or simply "The Breastplate Hymn") is one of the oldest hymns of the Christian church, dating to around 400 C.E. In its original form, it is a very lengthy creedal hymn on the Trinity and if used at all it is usually done so out of a sense of obligation rather than joy. However, this adaptation by James Quinn set to the familiar tune BUNNESAN ("Morning Has Broken," UMH, 145) makes this important hymn accessible to every congregation.

"Christ Beside Me" could be used as a regular hymn in any service dealing with faith and facing adversity. In addition, the hymn could be used effectively as a response at the end of a service, for example as a benediction response. This hymn would be an appropriate charge for Christians going out into the world facing the daily rigors of life. Since it is short and the melody is generally familiar, the hymn would be easy to memorize. Consequently, this hymn could serve as a "shield" for Christians as they go about their daily business. The catchy melody will bring the text to mind throughout the day, offering comfort and courage.

Christ has risen (2115)

Themes: Christ's Resurrection; Easter

This is a marvelous hymn for use on Easter Sunday and makes a refreshing change from long-used familiar hymns. Although the tune, HOLY MANNA, appears in *The United Methodist Hymnal* (UMH, 150), it may be unfamiliar to many congregations. It consists of four phrases, three of which are exactly the same. Congregations who are adverse to learning new tunes will find this one particularly painless. Teach the tune by using a call and response technique: the song leader sings each phrase (four-measure groups) and then asks the congregation to respond.

Once the tune has been learned, congregations will discover this to be an altogether delightful hymn. The text by John Bell contains powerful images surrounding the Resurrection of Christ, which are presented in an unexpected, yet beautiful way. Take advantage of the grouping of the stanzas by having the women sing the second stanza and the men sing the third stanza. All should sing the first and last stanzas. The high voices of the choir or a soloist can sing the descant during the final stanza. If parts are sung, the original accompaniment should be used. For congregations who sing parts well, it is a nice change to sing at least one stanza *a cappella*. It would be appropriate to sing the final stanza in unison with the descant using the alternate accompaniment.

Christ the Lord is risen (2116)

Themes: Resurrection; Easter Sunday; praise of Christ

Tom Colvin's Easter text added to this Ghanian folk song is a natural expression of Easter joy. Sing this unaccompanied if possible and with the use of West African percussion, such as a shaker (maraca-type instrument or gourd with beads strung on the outside), drum, and a gong (cowbell-type sound). You may want a leader to sing the first measure as a solo and then invite the congregation to join on the remainder of each stanza. By doing this, the congregation can hear the text and free their hands and eyes from the printed page, entering into the singing with clapping and swaying.

This song may be used as an acclamation following the Easter Gospel lesson or as a "Hallelujah" at any other time appropriate for such a response. In the African spirit, other texts can be added: "Death, where is thy sting?" (1 Cor. 15:55); "Christ will come again" (Ascension); "The stone was rolled away" (Matt. 28:2); and so forth. It would also be an excellent processional song for the choir on Easter Sunday.

Clap your hands (2028)

Themes: Praise; singing; celebration; the greatness of God

This exuberant song calls the congregation to celebrate the greatness of God through clapping their hands and singing a new song.

The choir or praise team could sing the song through the first time as a call to worship. Then the congregation could join on the repeat. The suggested hand claps add to the feeling of celebration. Using percussion could help the congregation with the hand claps and reinforce the overall rhythmic feel. This song calls for a brisk tempo of approximately 120-130 beats per minute.

Come, all you people (2274)
Uyai Mose
Themes: Gathering; praise

This is an entrance song for worship in the Shona tradition of Zimbabwe. This song may be accompanied by a *hosho* (a maraca-type shaker with seeds inside) playing eighth note patterns. A light drum is possible, but not necessary. A simple swaying is also part of the response to the song. Begin by learning the melody. Then add the tenor (sopranos may sing the tenor part an octave above as well). The two-note bass part is a favorite of men in the congregation. They will delight in singing it with only a brief rehearsal. The solo part is intended to encourage the congregation to join in the singing and should increase intensity upon repetition. Sing at least four times until all feel the unity of singing and swaying together.

The Shona takes very little effort for the congregation to learn because of its repetition. Singing the song in Shona adds variety to the repeated cycles. This song was written originally for children and is an ideal intergenerational selection for all choirs to sing on a choir dedication Sunday. Sing unaccompanied if at all possible.

Come and fill our hearts (2157)
Confitemini Domino
Themes: Peace; presence of God; thanksgiving; assurance; mystery of God

This is one of the most effective Taizé Community selections, from a monastic order situated in a tiny village in southeastern France. In this case the Latin and English have different meanings. The Latin text means literally, "I confess the Lord who is good." The English text establishes a petition for the Lord to "come and fill our hearts." Sing unaccompanied if possible. Additional instrumental parts are available in the Accompaniment Edition. A guitar accompaniment with cello support is very effective.

This song can be used effectively as a centering song at the beginning of worship or as a call to prayer. Sing it at least four times for it to have sufficient time to draw the community into prayer. In the Taizé Community, a selection such as this might be repeated over thirty times, allowing the singer to move away from the written music and to offer individual prayers above the song.

Come and fill our homes (2188)

Themes: Festival of the Christian Home; family; thanksgiving; blessing a household

"The Family Prayer Song" is a wonderful message of commitment from a family or household to God. It would be suitable on Mother's Day or Father's Day as well as Thanksgiving Sunday or Thanksgiving Wednesday. It would also work well for a Service for the Blessing of a Home (*The United Methodist Book of Worship*, 610). Sing this song before embarking upon the ritual of blessing.

As with most short praise choruses, you can extend the song by repeating portions of it, or by reading scripture in the midst of it. When doing so, sing the song in its entirety, then keep the music going while you read the scripture. Sing the song again, repeating it several times for each reading. Three scripture passages to consider would be Matthew 7:24; Mark 3:25; and John 14:2.

Come and find the quiet center (2128)

Themes: Inner peace; serenity

This hymn will be cherished by those who value quiet meditation and private devotion and by those seeking the calming presence of the Spirit amid a life of "chaos and clutter." It could be used as a tool for directed prayer and meditation, perhaps in a Service of Evening Prayer (*The United Methodist Hymnal*, 878). This might be done during the Silence immediately following the Scripture reading. As the organ or piano plays the hymn quietly, perhaps with a soft solo instrument playing the melody, the worship leader can speak all or selected phrases of the hymn text, allowing for a period of silent prayer following each phrase. The congregation could conclude this directed prayer by singing the hymn in its entirety. Another use of this hymn would be to extract almost any of its four-measure phrases and use it as a sung, repeated meditation in the manner of the Taizé Community.

Come and see (2127)

Kyrie

Theme: Call to follow Christ

This short hymn, partially based on Jesus' calling the first disciples in John 1, can be used to begin worship, as an invitation to Christian discipleship, as a baptism hymn, or as service music Kyrie. Both of the two parts (melody and descant) can be sung by children's choirs. The descant could be replaced or doubled by a solo instrument, such as the flute or violin. Older youth or adult choirs may want to add a simple bass part by singing almost all of each line on a tonic D, with a dominant A to end lines 1 and 3, and a dominant A and final D in the last measure of lines 2 and 4. It would be a simple matter to add handbell chords in D, G, and A major at the point of those harmonic changes.

With a little preparation and rhythmic alteration, choirs and congregations can substitute alternate English for the Greek. *Kyrie:* "Lord, have mercy"; *Kyrie eleison:* "Lord, have mercy upon us"; *Christe:* "Christ, have mercy"; *Christe elei-*

son: "Christ, have mercy upon us"; *Christe, Christe, adoramus te:* "Jesus Christ, we adore you."

Come as a child (2252)
Theme: Baptism

This text may be used as an invitation at the beginning of the baptismal covenant. It can be sung as each candidate comes forward for baptism, or once before or after all candidates are presented.

Care should be taken to preserve the rhythmic pattern of the tune. A slight *ritard* in the last three measures works well musically. A simple guitar accompaniment is also effective.

Come away with me (2202)
Themes: Holy Spirit; prayer; contemplation; Jesus at prayer

The voice of the Holy Spirit calls us in this hymn to prayer and reflection. After the opening stanza of invitation to prayer, the second stanza reminds us of the places where Jesus took time to pray. The third stanza is one of praise and thanksgiving; the fourth speaks of confession; and the fifth sings of God's grace.

The entire hymn might be used as a call to prayer or reflection on prayer. At those times, let the third stanza be sung in parts by the choir, and then the descant on the fourth stanza. Or alternate the stanzas with spoken or unspoken prayers, while the music is played throughout, matching the spoken prayers to the concerns just sung. Flute may double the melody and play an additional stanza during the silent prayer time.

Come, Be Baptized (2252)
See "Come as a child."

Come! Come! Everybody worship (2271)
Vengan Todos Adoremos
Themes: Opening of worship; Sabbath; rest; thanksgiving; prayer

The major movements of any worship service are noted in the stanzas of this simple song. Originally written for children, it is appealing to singers of all ages. A creative preacher or children's church leader can find a "sermon" in the stanzas about the parts of worship. We set aside a time to worship, worship calls us to help others, we offer our gifts to God in worship, we pray in worship, and finally, we learn how to live our lives as God's people.

Use a soloist or group of children on the stanzas, with everyone singing the refrain. The tempo should be sprightly ($\quarternote$ = 84-88). Encourage non-Spanish-speaking singers to try the Spanish refrain.

Come, Holy Spirit (2125)

Themes: Holy Spirit; Pentecost; invitation

This is a versatile song in that it would fit with many different parts of a worship service. The text is an invitation to the Holy Spirit to join the community in worship, to bless those who are seeking understanding, truth, and ways to glorify God. It is appropriate for the beginning of a worship service, as a first song of an opening praise medley. It is also appropriate for the last song of an opening praise medley, inviting the Spirit to come and reside during the hour of praise. It can be used as a preparation for a scripture reading, the message, or a time of prayer. Use the song both before and after the segment for which you choose it as a frame. This song may be sung as a response to the benediction or dismissal, inviting the Spirit to walk with us every day. If used at this point in the service, follow it with another, more upbeat closing song.

Come, let us with our Lord arise (2084)

Theme: Resurrection

This joyous English folk melody takes on a triumphant character when wed to this Easter text by Charles Wesley. Effective as a congregational hymn, it may also serve as an Easter introit for the choir. The first phrase of stanza 2 might be used as a sung response to the Easter Sunday psalm (Psalm 118, UMH, 839).

The melodic structure of the first three lines of this hymn allows for two, three, or four trumpets to play this melody in canon, with each trumpet entering at one-measure intervals. Optional keyboard accompaniment can be added, consisting of F major and B♭ major chords alternating every two beats above a sustained F pedal point. The last two lines might be played with improvised parallel thirds. This arrangement could be used as an introduction to either the choral introit or congregational hymn.

Come! Live in the light! (2172)

Themes: Social holiness; discipleship; justice; love; service; kingdom building

This hymn is a wonderful setting of the Micah 6:8 call to walk with God humbly, doing justice, loving mercy, and serving one another. The refrain might be taught to the congregation first, with soloists or choir on the stanzas, but soon the congregation will be able to sing it all. It is appropriate for times of discipleship, commitment, and invitation to justice and social ministries. It might also be sung during the distribution of communion as a reminder of the life to which Christ calls us.

When first teaching this hymn, keep a quarter note beat in the left-hand accompaniment and straight chording. Add the triplet figures and additional flourishes in the accompaniment after the congregation is more familiar with the tune. Consider using this hymn for ecumenical services and during the Week for Christian Unity.

Come now, O Prince of Peace (2232)
O-So-So

Themes: Prayer; petition; Advent; unity; hope; political and spiritual freedom

Geonyong Lee is a prominent Korean composer and church musician. He wrote this song as a plea for unity among Christians and in the hope that his war-torn and politically divided Korean homeland might be unified some day. It is beautiful when sung unaccompanied, but can be supported by a light organ accompaniment with strings. The melody is in a Korean folk style that is quite accessible.

Consider singing this song throughout the Advent season, adding a stanza each Sunday. It is also an appropriate hymn to use following the prayers for the world. Another possibility is to sing each stanza separately and to place a brief spoken prayer of unity and hope between the stanzas. World Communion Sunday also is a potentially effective day to sing this song. As a petition, join it closely with spoken prayers. Many communities have Korean congregations. They may not know this song, but will be pleased to learn it. A version with Korean characters can be found in *Global Praise I*, a collection of world songs published by the General Board of Global Ministries. This is the most effective way to introduce it to Korean speakers, rather than through the transliteration provided in this collection. English-speaking congregations can learn to sing this song in Korean from the transliteration because of the slow pace and repetition of the text. Invite a Korean Christian to teach your choir the Korean pronunciation.

Come, O Holy Spirit, come (2124)
Wa Wa Wa Emimimo

Themes: Pentecost; power of the Holy Spirit; invocation

This Nigerian song is very popular among the Yoruba tribe, one of the major tribal groups in western Africa. The song is in the Yoruba language and is used widely among all Christians. It may be taught easily by a prepared leader without any books in hand, even in the Yoruba language. A common practice among the Yoruba is to extend their arms fully upward and bring down the Holy Spirit on their heads as they sing *Wa* (the imperative form of the verb "to come"). An "o" added on to the end of a verb in Yoruba doubles its strength. Thus, *wao* adds an urgency to the imperative verb—"come *now*, Lord."

A simple congregational movement would involve a small step at the beginning of each measure: small step right, close with left foot; small step left, close with right foot. This step would take one measure. As you close with both the left or right foot, add a clap. Sing unaccompanied if possible and use West African percussion, such as a shaker (maraca-type instrument or gourd with beads strung on the outside), drum, and a gong (cowbell-type sound). Use this song as an invocation of the Holy Spirit or as a processional at the beginning of worship, a common African practice. Sing in a lively and rhythmic fashion. Maintain the beat right to the end of the song without slowing down.

Come, rejoice in God (2017)
Jubilate Servite
Themes: Praise; gratitude; thanksgiving; offering for service

This paraphrase of Psalm 100 is one of the most popular canons sung in the Taizé Community, an ecumenical monastic community in France. This is a lively song that may work better if felt in two beats per measure, rather than four. The Latin is relatively simple and many congregations may enjoy trying this venerable language of the church. "Come, Rejoice in God" may be supported by a simple two-measure keyboard ostinato pattern (repeated rhythmic and melodic figure) and/or other instruments, such as guitar, oboe, cello, and trumpet.

Sing as a response to psalms of praise, such as Psalms 100, 117, or 150. This song may serve also as a processional for the choir with a simple handbell ostinato taken from the "Hallelujah" measures in the last two lines of the music. If the choir steps faithfully to the half note, they can stay together—even in canon. Consider using this song during a festive season of the Christian Year, such as the month of November or one of the Sundays after Easter. Sing in unison for a few Sundays and then try it in canon. Following a brief congregational rehearsal before the service, the congregation will enjoy singing in a two- or three-part round if the choir is prepared to lead them. Consider singing it as a song of gratitude when bringing the offering forward.

For a more exciting musical effect, start the canon at one-measure intervals instead of four measures.

Come, Share the Lord (2269)
See "We gather here in Jesus' name."

Come to the table (2264)
Themes: Invitation to communion; statement of faith; provision

This beautiful invitation to communion could be used at several points in the service. Consider singing it several times during a communion service (e.g., opening, a quiet worship medley, while communion elements are being prepared). It is very effective to have interpretive dancers bring the communion elements to the altar while the song is being sung and/or played. Keep the melody very *legato* and at a fairly slow tempo ($\downarrow$. = 52-56).

As a conclusion, repeat the phrase "Come at the Lord's invitation." This song works well with "I Come with Joy" (UMH, 617). As a bridge between the songs, play an introduction that increases the tempo and changes the style from *legato* to somewhat detached and bouncy.

Communion Setting (2257)

Theme: The Great Thanksgiving

This setting of responses for use in the Great Thanksgiving prayer at celebrations of Word and Table might be called the "Hosanna" setting, for Mark A. Miller returns to that theme again and again. The first of these provides music for the opening dialogue (called the Sursum Corda from the line "Lift up your hearts"). The presiding minister sings the leader's part. Because the presider's part is limited to one note (except for the last note), it is an easy part for presiders who are less comfortable with singing alone. A presider with a gift for chanting or improvisation can sing the entire preface if desired. The Sanctus introduces us to the "Hosanna" theme, which reappears in both the "Memorial Acclamation" and the "Amen."

In learning the responses, a call and response format may be used. One effective variation is to have a solo voice sing the first "Hosanna in the highest," with the choir singing the second, and the entire congregation the third. When sung in unison throughout, each of the three "Hosanna" phrases should build in intensity and volume.

Confitemini Domino (2157)

See "Come and fill our hearts."

Cry of My Heart (2165)

See "It is the cry of my heart."

Da Pacem Cordium (2156)

See "Give peace."

Deep in the shadows of the past (2246)

Themes: Holy Scriptures; salvation history; persons of faith throughout history

This hymn gives praise for the stories of faith passed on to us in the Scriptures. It sings of how God has been at work, beginning with the Hebrew people and the promises of "I AM WHAT I WILL BE" through days of Pentecost. Sing it anytime to celebrate the gifts of Scripture, giving Bibles to young people, or the beginning or end of a Bible study group. Work with the text in a study group about the complexities and wonderful riches of how we came to receive the Bible.

The English folk tune is easily taught, as three of the four lines are identical, except for their final note. In the beginning, play the melody in octaves or on an instrument, without the accompaniment. Then add the flowing accompaniment and sing with strength.

Dios Está Aquí (2049)
See "God is here today."

Earth Prayer (2059)
See "I am your mother."

Enviado Soy de Dios (2184)
See "Sent out in Jesus' name."

Eres Digno (2063)
See "You are worthy."

Eternal Father, strong to save (2191)
Themes: God's providential care; trust in God; safety in time of danger

This hymn, commonly known as "The Navy Hymn," is not at all militaristic. It is a prayer cry to the triune God "for those in peril on the sea" and for all travelers in danger. It is a fitting hymn whenever a congregation has a reason to remember sailors, merchant mariners, fishermen, and others who go to sea—especially if they are on dangerous missions. Its invocation of each person of the Trinity in turn and then to the Triune God, relating each to the sea, can stimulate reflection. A congregation already conscious of the dangers they or their loved ones face at sea may be ready to sing it as an opening hymn. If the preaching calls attention to those in peril, this hymn may follow as a response. It may precede or follow a scripture reading, such as Jesus stilling the storm. It is most effective sung in four-part harmony.

Some hymnals wed this MELITA tune to the familiar text: "My hope is built on nothing less than Jesus' blood and righteousness. . . . On Christ the solid rock I stand" (UMH, 368), which provides a very different and effective setting of this text.

Every promise we can make (2162)
Themes: Grace; assurance; courage; hope

The text of this song clearly states that it is only by God's grace that we are able to live an abundant life. The authors/composers show us specific examples of God's grace in our daily lives. The beautifully flowing ($\quarternote$ = 88-96) and very singable melody will be easy to teach to any congregation. There is an optional choral ending that might be sung by a praise team or choir. It repeats the refrain two times while adding harmonizing parts for a climactic ending.

This song can be used at any point in a service where assurance of God's care for us is the emphasis. A soloist might introduce the song, or divide the stanzas or eight-measure phrases between several soloists. If soloists are being used as well as the choral ending, have a soloist sing the very last phrase: "We will go forth in grace alone."

Faith is patience in the night (2211)
Theme: Faith

This simple hymn is a testimony of faith in a variety of settings: patience, joy, pain, stress, and hopelessness. It should be sung in a slow and serene manner, not at all rushed. For the most part, the tune is simple and straightforward. The unexpected intervals in the second measure may prove challenging and may require some planning before introducing the hymn to the congregation. For example, the choir could sing it as part of the service music, the organist could play it as an offertory, and so on. If a congregational rehearsal is necessary, try singing just the first phrase several times as a call and response: the song leader sings the phrase and the congregation answers.

The hymn could be used appropriately on any occasion where a hymn on faith is needed.

Father, I adore you (2038)
Themes: Adoration; praise to the Trinity; commitment; surrender

This is a very familiar song in many worshiping communities, and it is easy to teach to those unfamiliar with it. Sung as a canon, it is truly beautiful in its simplicity and sound. Have your vocal team or choir lead the congregation as one unit to get everyone singing together. Then have a few voices in your choir or vocal team begin the canon after you have gone through the song in its entirety. As people feel comfortable with the song, they will join in the canon.

If you want the text to reflect a spirit of community rather than individual praise, change the personal pronouns from singular to plural ("Father, *we* adore you"). Consider following this song with an upbeat praise tune, especially one with some lively instrumentation, such as "King of Kings" (2075), or something powerful, such as "Shout to the Lord" (2074).

Father, we love you (2016)
Themes: Praise; adoration; praise to the Trinity

This chorus makes a good ending for a praise medley. Keep the tempo fairly slow (about ♩ = 84). Consider lighting altar candles for each person of the Trinity as the congregation sings each verse. When the last verse has been completed, repeat the last section of the song (from the repeated "Glorify thy name"), and during this repeat, greatly reduce the volume and intensity of the accompaniment, so that the worshipers can connect at a deeper level. If this song is used in a praise medley, use the set to precede a time of prayer, the offering, or the sermon. Repeat this song later in the service, perhaps as a response to the sermon.

For all the saints (2283)

Themes: Adoration and praise; All Saints Day; a new heaven and a new earth

This hymn by John Bell would be an excellent alternative to William How's "For All the Saints." Where Ralph Vaughan Williams's setting, SINE NOMINE, is vigorous and festively rhythmical, and is suitable for a processional or recessional, this hymn is set to the familiar English folk tune O WALY WALY and is more quiet and contemplative. You would not necessarily have to choose between the two hymns because their settings are so different. Both hymns could be used together in the same service commemorating All Saints Day.

This hymn could also be used to commemorate the hard work and service of various people (known and unknown) within a church community.

For One Great Peace (2185)

See "This thread I weave."

Forgive us, Lord (2134)

Perdón, Señor

Themes: Confession; repentance; forgiveness

This song is to be sung in a call and response fashion. It may be used as a prayer of confession. The congregation may sing the short refrain ("Forgive us, Lord") while the leader sings the petitions. The leader may want to read the petitions instead, thus allowing him or her to lift up other areas of concern. Alternately, the choir may sing the refrain and the congregation the petitions. If the choir sings the refrain, they may want to consider holding the last chord while petitions are being sung or read.

Encourage the congregation to sing the refrain in Spanish as well as in English, repeating it several times at the end of the piece, while gradually *decrescendo*.

This song is appropriate for the Lenten Season, especially during Holy Week. It is also particularly appropriate for Peace with Justice Sunday. Suggested tempo: ($\downarrow$ = 69).

Freedom Is Coming (2192)

See "O freedom" (South Africa).

From the rising of the sun (2024)

Themes: Praise and adoration of God

Through the repetitious use of these words in the Psalms (mouth, praise, declare, sing, lips, tongue), we learn that praise is to be expressed openly in the congregation and not only as quiet, personal thoughts. This song is a good example of an open expression of praise that gathers the people to worship. It is a moderate tempo ($\downarrow$ = 92).

This might be the first song in a medley of several praise songs. Possible songs to include: "I Sing Praises to Your Name" (2037); "Lord, I Lift Your Name on High" (2088); and "My Life Is in You, Lord" (2032). Another option would be to sing the song one time, read related scripture, and then sing it again. This pattern could be repeated several times throughout a service that has been designed around the different aspects of praise. This song is also appropriate for Services of Morning or Evening Praise and Prayer (UMH, 876 and 878).

Gather Us In (2236)
See "Here in this place."

Give me a clean heart (2133)
Theme: Confession
In this setting of Psalm 51:10 (with a concluding affirmation of steadfast loyalty), Margaret Douroux engages singers in what can be considered a "purging process through the music." Thus, it should be sung quite slowly and with deep feeling. It is most appropriately placed before the prayer of confession or between the confession and the words of assurance.

Give peace (2156)
Da Pacem Cordium
Themes: Peace; reconciliation; presence of God; assurance
Canons are a common musical form in the Taizé Community, an ecumenical monastic movement in France. A primary theme of the community is reconciliation. This song communicates this theme in a simple, but powerful manner. As suggested in the score, the congregation may sing by centering on a single pitch. Instrumentalists and/or vocal soloists may sing above this single pitch, adding interest and variety. Unison singing is a symbol of unity in the New Testament. Singing on a single pitch allows even the most insecure singers to participate.

Use as a preparation for morning prayer or congregational intercessory prayer. After several services, the congregation may be ready to try the song as a canon if supported by the choir. Singing in canon is an effective way to increase the congregation's sense of musical competence and adds variety to traditional Western hymnody in a stanza form. The Latin is simple to sing and can contribute to a sense of the mystery of God.

Give thanks with a grateful heart (2036)
Themes: Thanksgiving; praise and adoration of God
This very popular and beautiful contemporary song focuses our hearts on the infinite goodness of God and the joy of pouring out our appreciation to God.

It can be used at any point in the service but would be particularly appropriate as a framework for the time of offering or response to the spoken word. It can begin with a small ensemble singing the first three phrases (measures 1-8) and then the congregation singing the repeat of those phrases (measures 9-16); or three soloists can sing the first three phrases followed by a small ensemble or congregation.

If the song is used to begin a service based on thanksgiving, include a call to worship or responsive reading based on corresponding scriptures. This is a moderately flowing piece (♩ = 96) that could be beautifully interpreted by dance.

Gloria a Dios (2033)
See "Glory to God."

Glorify Thy Name (2016)
See "Father, we love you."

Glory to God (2033)
Gloria a Dios
Theme: Praise to the Trinity

This invigorating song from Peru invites us to praise the Trinity with our whole being. It is set in a call and response pattern, with the song leader singing first and the people responding. Because of the nature of the rhythm, the congregation may need to learn the tune first, using a syllable such as "lah" and singing a phrase at a time, until they feel comfortable with the tune. This tune also invites body movement. The congregation may be encouraged to sway slightly as they sing. This works well as a praise song, or as a response to the Word. It is particularly appropriate for Trinity Sunday.

It may be sung as indicated for "leader" and "all," or you may divide the congregation in two. One side will sing the part of the leader and the other side will sing where "all" is indicated. The last two lines could be sung as they appear, with leader/congregation. The choir would be very helpful as they gradually build the D minor chord as indicated in the music.

This song is most effective using percussion instrument(s) only. Suggested tempo: (♩ = 96).

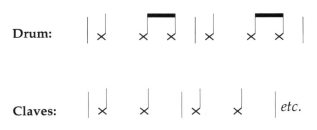

Glory to God in the highest (2276)
Theme: Praise and adoration

From David Haas's well-loved *Mass of Light* comes this excerpt from the "Great Gloria" (the Gloria in Excelsis), so-called to distinguish it from the Gloria Patri. It is most effective to have the congregation sing the refrain and the choir or song leader sing the verses (included in the Accompaniment and Singer's Editions). Although especially appropriate at Christmas, it is a song of praise that was often used at Services of Holy Communion in various Methodist traditions. The complete Mass setting may be used in celebration of Holy Communion. Vocal parts, including a sung presider's part, are available from GIA Publications.

The use of percussion adds to the intensity and dynamism of this response. The held notes provide marvelous opportunities for instrumental improvisation.

Go ye, go ye into the world (2239)
Themes: Missions; evangelism; gospel proclamation

This song can be sung on numerous occasions when the theme is missions, preaching the gospel, or world outreach, and certainly for an ordination service. Jesus' calling of the disciples and commissioning them to go out two by two is a favorite story of young children, and this song will reinforce that theme in a Sunday school class.

It exhibits a lively, almost dancelike quality, suggested by the light syncopation of the eighth notes. It is simple enough that even a young children's handbell or chime choir could play it as a prelude or to accompany singing. Orff instruments could also be effectively used here. Melody and descant lines are simple enough that the congregation can learn both of them, and various divisions of the voices could be used. A third voice part for men's voices could be improvised, consisting of all half notes alternating on G and D, singing repetitions of "Go ye," with a whole note "Go" in the final bar. This would be especially effective if women's voices divided the melody and descant lines between them.

God Claims You (2249)
See "Child of promise."

God, how can we forgive (2169)
Themes: Forgiveness; confession; grace

The first stanza is a wrenching cry from those who have suffered the abuse or rupture of a loving relationship It speaks most fully when there is a sense of fault on both sides, for if stanza 1 reflects the cry of one wronged, stanza 2 speaks of the wrong one has done. Stanza 3 can be understood as the prayer of the community (as well as the individuals involved), celebrating God's grace and forgiveness. This hymn may be used in services of healing and reconcilia-tion, or when one or both partners are seeking to take appropriate (but not total) responsibility for the end of a covenant relationship.

Care must be taken, however, not to use it inappropriately. In an age that all too often blames the victim and seeks to move toward forgiveness of per-petrators prematurely, stanzas 2 and 3 could add to the sense of failure and guilt on the part of the abused person.

The strong tune will be familiar to congregations who sing "The God of Abraham Praise" (UMH, 116). However, for this text, accompanists should use a softer registration with a solo stop to contribute to the reflective nature of these words.

God is here today (2049)
Dios Está Aquí
Themes: Assurance of God's presence; God's faithfulness

This traditional song from Mexico is an affirmation of confidence and trust in the very real presence of God in our midst, as we gather for worship, as we go about our daily lives. It is a good reminder that God is with us "in every breath we take."

It is appropriate for morning worship, as a call to worship, or response to prayer.

It might first be introduced by a flutist playing the melody line, accomp-anied by simple, strummed guitar chords.

Take this at a moderate tempo, allowing the congregation to feel the music, "taste" the words, and praise and greet God through the song. Suggested tempo: ($\quad$ = 64).

God is so good (2056)
Themes: God's providential care; praise and thanksgiving

This simple chorus slips quickly into the people's memory banks and has various uses. Sung as printed, it fits easily into an opening praise service or med-ley of praise choruses. As an acclamation of joy and praise, the first stanza can be planned or spontaneously volunteered as a response to good news—easily sung without accompaniment, though easy for the accompanist to join even when spontaneous. It works well as a communion song when many of the peo-ple are standing or kneeling and unable to use a hymnal or look at a screen. The leader can call out the simple four-syllable stanzas as printed or improvise other stanzas to fit the occasion. The leader may even call out a change in the final phrase—such as changing "me" to "us," or ending, "God is good, so good."

This chorus is especially effective with a soft solo instrument (flute, violin, oboe) accompanied by keyboard. Because of its simple harmony, a children's or beginning handbell choir could easily learn to play it. The simple and beau-tiful harmonies lend themselves to a cappella choir singing.

God made from one blood (2170)
Themes: Nurturing families; the human family; Festival of the Christian Home

This hymn recognizes the importance of the family unit bound by blood relation as well as a wider extended family that includes others who offer nurture and support traditionally offered by true family. It recognizes that family life may not always be peaceful and loving, and may even do harm. It is a prayer to transform and heal our families and restore relationships, and to do the same for the entire human family.

This hymn would be appropriate on many significant occasions within an individual's or family's life: birth, baptism, confirmation, and marriage. Also, it allows a congregation to offer words of hope and encouragement at those times when families in the local church or community are in need of prayers and support. It is also appropriate for the observance of the Festival of the Christian Home.

The text is best supported with a minimum of musical creativity to detract from its seriousness.

God the sculptor of the mountains (2060)
Themes: Creation; baptism; communion; confirmation; God of the Old Testament; Jesus Christ; praise; prayer

This wonderful praise hymn is full of images from the Old Testament, from the life of Jesus Christ, and from our lives as Christians. The final line of each stanza is a prayer that God will shape us, lead us, feed us, and meet us.

Add a string or electric bass, and let the rhythm chords (thinking four beats to the measure) be strong. This will add energy to the melody, which moves easily in steps. Percussion instruments are very appropriate and clapping may also be added. This hymn may easily become a favorite as it is so rich in biblical images of God. It would be a good study hymn for confirmation, or for any Sunday school class from older elementary up through senior citizens.

God weeps (2048)
Themes: Social justice; child abuse; anti-violence; compassion

This hauntingly beautiful hymn by Shirley Erena Murray with setting by Carlton R. Young touches on social issues that are not often addressed in hymnody: child abuse, physical violence toward women, and cruelty to animals. The tune may be difficult for some congregations to learn because of the complex harmonies of the accompaniment. However, the melody has a naturally repeating sequence, which actually makes the tune rather easy to learn and sing. The last two notes of the tune are also the same as the first two notes. Consequently, there is a natural feel as the melody progresses from stanza to stanza. The unresolved harmony in the accompaniment at the end of the hymn adds to the mysterious quality of the setting, creating a kind of text and musical painting depicting God weeping, bleeding, and waiting.

It would probably be best initially to teach this hymn without the accompaniment while playing along with the melody in unison octaves. Once the congregation is familiar and comfortable with the tune, the accompaniment can be added to great effect.

Goodness is stronger than evil (2219)
Themes: Assurance; overcoming evil; victory through Christ

John Bell, the chief musician of the Iona Community in Scotland, has provided an effective setting of a prayer by South African Anglican Bishop Desmond Tutu. It comes from the context of black South African's struggle against the evil, racist system of apartheid. Sing firmly and with energy that builds throughout the selection, especially at the text "Victory is ours." Do not slow down until the end.

This selection can be used as a response to any scripture that demonstrates the power of Christ over evil, such as the healing of the demoniac (Matt. 9:32-34); the temptations of Christ in the wilderness (Matt. 4:7); and the greatest triumph—the Resurrection of Christ. Brief prayers might be offered that call the church to be a witness against evil in the present world. This song can be sung as a response to each prayer. It is not intended to be repeated in the fashion of Taizé songs, but as a response to specific petitions or prayers of thanksgiving in which Christ's power over evil should be recognized. If played on the organ, use a bright registration and a detached style. When possible, sing unaccompanied or with a light piano or guitar accompaniment for support.

Grace Alone (2162)
See "Every promise we can make."

Gracias, Señor (2044)
See "My gratitude now accept, O God."

Great is the Lord (2022)
Themes: Adoration; praise; God's majesty and power; God's faithfulness

This Michael W. Smith chorus serves as a great service opener. The lilting 6/8 meter and easy-to-sing melody make it a favorite of people of all ages. Use it to begin a medley of praise and worship songs and then repeat the last fourteen measures at the end of the medley. You can also take the last fourteen measures and sing "to God" by changing the pronouns. Sing "Great are you, Lord, and worthy of glory! I lift up my voice: Great are you, Lord!" and so forth.

The Singer's and Accompaniment Editions have parts for a choir or ensemble, including an optional choral ending.

Guide my feet (2208)

Themes: Prayer for strength, support

Historically, the tempo of this spiritual ranges from moderately slow to lively, depending upon the congregation and the location of the song as an act of worship in the order of service. With the assistance of other worship leaders, the musician should determine the tempo and introduce the spiritual to the choir and congregation, with or without instrumentation, using the harmony as indicated in the score.

The text is appropriate as a response to scripture, such as Hebrews 12:1-2 or Psalm 139:23-24 (stanza 5). Use it also as a sung prayer during prayers for healing and wholeness or prayers for strength in times of trials (stanzas 2 and 3) or as a call to confession (stanza 5). It can be effectively used with movement by the congregation or by a liturgical dance group.

Halle, Halle, Halleluja (2026-a, 2026-b)

Themes: Praise; thanksgiving; gratitude

This lively, rhythmic Caribbean tune can be sung after only one hearing. Its syncopated melody lends itself to clapping and swaying to the beat. A simple congregational movement would involve a small step at the beginning of each measure: small step right, close with left foot; small step left, close with right foot. This step would take the first four measures. As you close with both the left or right foot, add a clap. Children and young people will immediately respond, and others will enjoy trying even if they are not entirely successful at first. Add tambourine, maracas, claves, and bongos. Give each one a different pattern. A guitar or piano, rather than the organ, provides the best accompaniment.

Sing as a response to the Gospel lesson or to appropriate psalm selections, such as Psalms 95, 96, 98, 100, 117, or 150. It is quite common to adapt the text slightly to fit the occasion. For example, sing the doxology to this tune while presenting the congregation's tithes and offerings:

Praise to God from whom all blessings flow.
Praise to God all creatures here below.
Praise to God above ye heav'nly hosts.
Hallelujah, Hallelujah.

(Thomas Ken, adapt.)

Carlton R. Young's arrangement (2026-b) of this tune provides additional verses and performance options.

Harvest Song (2061)

See "Praise our God above."

He came down (2085)

Themes: Praise; Advent; Incarnation; love; peace; joy

This simple, declarative statement from Cameroon may be most fitting during the Advent season. Use it on the four Sundays during Advent as the candles on the Advent wreath are lit. In many churches the themes are hope, peace, joy, and love on the four successive Sundays of this season. Each Sunday a stanza would be added until the fourth Sunday would include all of the themes of Advent. Note the leader's part that asks the question, "Why did he come?" This is an important feature of the African style. Another possibility is for the leader to anticipate the key word in the next stanza at this point, for example, "Christ brought us hope." The congregation would then follow with "He came down that we might have hope." Of course, the acknowledgment of the Christ's coming is not limited to Advent. Other nouns may be substituted and indicated by the leader: grace, light, life, and so on.

As in other African selections, movement is appropriate, especially a gentle swaying; and percussion can be added, including a shaker (maraca-type instrument or gourd with beads strung on the outside), drum, and a gong (cowbell-type sound). Assign each a different pattern, creating a layered effect. Sing unaccompanied or with guitar or piano.

He Has Made Me Glad (2270)

See "I will enter his gates."

He is exalted (2070)

Themes: Christ's Lordship and reign; adoration and praise; God's majesty and power; Word of God

Twila Paris's "He Is Exalted" has become a praise and worship standard all around the world. With its flowing 6/8 meter, it sings well and can be accompanied by anything from pipe organ to a full praise band, and anything in between. After singing it once with the congregation, invite them to sing the chorus to God by changing the pronouns: "You are exalted, O King, you're exalted on high, I will praise you. You are exalted, forever exalted and I will praise your name. You are the Lord, forever your truth shall reign; heaven and earth rejoice in your holy name. You are exalted, O King, you're exalted on high." This song would also be appropriate for a processional complete with banners and liturgical dancers.

Sing this chorus in a medley of other hymns in praise of Christ. It is especially appropriate for celebrations of Christ's reign, such as Easter, Ascension Sunday, and Christ the King Sunday.

He who began a good work in you (2163)

Themes: God's faithfulness; assurance; ministry in daily life; commissioning to serve

This chorus, based on Philippians 1:6, reminds us that it is God who works in and through us. We can trust that God will be faithful to complete the work begun in our lives. This focus makes the song very appropriate for times of commissioning works of ministry, such as sending a mission team, ordination or consecration, or a congregational sending forth. For congregations concerned about clear and inclusive language, it is easy and comfortable to substitute "God" for the male pronouns.

Sing this at a relaxed tempo (♩ = 100). A simple finger-picked guitar and some light percussion (shakers, bongo drums) would nicely support the rhythm and style of the song. Repeat the refrain several times. After the congregation is comfortable with the song, some singers may echo the first, third and fourth phrases. Repeat the last phrase, "God who started a work" as an ending. Verses to this song may be found in *Renew! Songs & Hymns for Blended Worship* (Hope Publishing Company).

Healer of our every ill (2213)

Themes: Strength in tribulation; Holy Spirit; comfort; vision; healing; God's presence and grace

This prayer hymn reminds us that God is our healer, the One who holds tomorrow, who gives peace for fear and hope for sorrow. It calls upon the Holy Spirit for comfort, vision, guidance, and compassion. Introduce it by having the congregation speak and pray the refrain, as soloists sing the stanzas. Then teach the refrain first, and finally teach the stanzas. Use it as a call to prayer, in times of trial, at services of prayer and healing, and at funerals.

Let the tempo be gentle. Add guitar if desired, and the optional descant from the Accompaniment Edition. Two flutes or oboes could make a lovely duet from the refrain melody and descant.

Here am I (2178)

Themes: Social holiness; homeless persons; unemployed; justice ministries; communion; the call of Christ

This hymn speaks to us in the voice of Christ, who takes the side of the homeless, stands with persons in line for food, marches for justice, and calls us in the church to change our way of living. Although the tune is easy, the text challenges us to take our discipleship seriously and consider where we are.

Sing this as a call to commitment, using three soloists and slides of real people in your community or from around the world. Use it in the midst of a sermon, before communion, at a mission dinner, when considering housing the homeless in your church or helping at a food kitchen. Follow it with a chance for the congregation to respond, either in pledge of commitment or a creed. Keep the tempo thoughtful (♩ = 76).

Here in this place (2236)
Themes: Opening of worship; communion; unity; family of God

Gathering is essential to the Christian. We must be in community with one another and with God. This song asks God to create again a community that responds with thanks and praise.

"Gather Us In" can frame an entire worship service. Sing stanza 1 as a call to worship. Stanza 2 works well as a response to confession. Stanza 3 can be sung as the elements for communion are presented. Finally, stanza 4 can serve as a closing, reminding us of the greater gathering in God's kingdom.

Use a steady tempo that lets the eighth notes move along ($\downarrow$. = 56-64). Liturgical dancers can certainly enhance the singing of this hymn. Another performance idea would be to have the choir sing the first four phrases of each stanza (up to "light of this day" in stanza 1). Then the congregation may respond by singing the remainder of the stanza.

Here is bread, here is wine (2266)
Themes: Holy Communion; unity; sending forth

This is a new song to use during communion. Its text focuses on the offering of Jesus to humanity, and is an invitation to be in relationship with Jesus and with others. It is very simple, singable, and meditative. Play it with just a very simple guitar as accompaniment ($\downarrow$ = 68-76). A single voice leading the congregation in singing as people move forward for communion is very effective. Use this song as a first congregational song as the people move forward to receive communion. Use the last verse again at the end to send the people to be in ministry in the world after receiving the elements.

His Eye Is on the Sparrow (2146)
See "Why should I feel discouraged?"

Holy (2019)
Santo
Themes: God's faithfulness; God's care for God's children; ministry in daily life

This joyful song from the Salvadoran Popular Mass is an expression of praise and thanksgiving, written by the people to the God who lives and suffers with them in their daily journey. The union of faith and daily living is evident in other portions of the Mass.

This joy is reflected in the dancelike tune, which should be kept at a lively tempo ($\downarrow$ = 120). Start with a slower tempo while the congregation is learning the song (it may also be introduced by the choir or a small ensemble).

This song is appropriate for ordination or consecration services, with its theme of the proclamation of the good news (second stanza). It is appropriate for Pentecost Sunday.

Also, the first part of the song (without the repeat) could be used as part of the communion service music:

(Spoken): and so with your people on earth and all the company of heaven we praise your name and join their unending hymn:

(Sung): "Holy, holy . . . is our Lord, God is Lord of all creation, holy, holy is our Lord."

The accompaniment is more suitable for piano, but a guitar and bass guitar may be used.

Holy Ground (2272)

See "We are standing on holy ground."

Holy, holy (2039)

Themes: God's character; holiness; the Trinity; adoration; praise and thanksgiving

This well-loved song begins by focusing on God's holiness and ends by singing a "Hallelujah." In between there is a stanza giving thanks to each member of the Trinity. This song could function as a framework around which to structure the congregation's time of prayer, offering spoken prayers between the stanzas.

Because of the number of stanzas, "Holy, Holy" could benefit from alternating voices on the various stanzas. Guitar and/or keyboard accompaniment would serve this song well. The tempo should be relaxed, but not too slow, around 72 beats per minute.

Holy, holy, holy (2007)

Santo, Santo, Santo

Themes: Praise; thanksgiving; commitment

This hauntingly beautiful chorus from Argentina is a prayer offered to God from the heart of the believer, acknowledging the holiness of God. It is appropriate as a song of praise, as a commitment song, as a response to prayer, or as a response to the Word. Because the song is short, you may want to introduce it with a flute solo, along with some background accompaniment, then have the choir sing it once. Next, have the instruments (the flute and perhaps another instrument, adding a second voice) play it one more time, after which the congregation will sing the verse. Encourage the congregation to sing it in Spanish first, then in English. This will require some teaching time but the experience will also enrich congregational worship. This song works best at a slow pace. Suggested tempo: ($\downarrow$ = 69).

Holy, holy, holy Lord (2256)
Sanctus
Themes: Eucharist; praise

Sometimes called the "Iona Sanctus," this setting of the first response in the Great Thanksgiving Eucharistic prayer at first seems to be in a call and response format. However, that shifts to a unison approach in measures 3 and 4 and measures 7 and 8. In teaching the response, the call and response pattern may be continued by having the congregation continue to answer the call, thus repeating the two measures at those two points.

However, singing the response as at is written is recommended as soon as possible.

The song leader may take part 1 with the choir and the congregation singing part 2. When the response has been learned, the choir may join the song leader on part 1 with the congregation responding. This response will appeal to persons with diverse musical tastes and may serve as a unifying experience.

Holy Spirit, come to us (2118)
Veni Sancte Spiritus
Themes: Pentecost; healing; assurance

This is a simple ostinato that is used regularly in the Taizé Community, an ecumenical monastic order in France. This short fragment can be memorized almost immediately, freeing the worshiper to pray above the song. The Accompaniment Edition contains instrumental and song leader's parts that enhance this simple refrain. The song leader's parts quote scripture related to the power and work of the Holy Spirit and unobtrusively guide the worshiper's thoughts. The instrumental melodies are especially effective in establishing a wordless prayer. The support of a cello also increases the effectiveness of this petition.

Use on Pentecost Sunday in preparation for the reading from Acts. Use as an invocation at the beginning of the service or in preparation for a time of prayer. Creative song leaders can sing additional scriptures above the ostinato that are appropriate. The Latin can be sung more fluidly than the English and may be easily learned by the congregation.

Honor and Praise (2018)
See "Righteous and holy."

Hosanna! Hosanna! (2109)
See "Jesus rode into Jerusalem."

How Can I Keep from Singing (2212)
See "My life flows on."

How long, O Lord (2209)
Themes: Strength in tribulation; lament; wilderness times; God's constant grace

This text is based on one of the psalms of lament (Psalm 13), and the music has an appropriate "blues" character. It is a hymn that congregations will grow into, as they come to acknowledge the pain of life honestly before God and in turn receive reminders of God's grace and presence. This hymn would be appropriate whenever Psalm 13 appears in the lectionary, during Lent, and also, with careful use, at funerals or services of prayer and healing. Always acknowledge its positive words in the third stanza as people begin to move beyond grief and tribulation to take strength in God.

Set the tempo by considering the measure of constant eighth notes (measure 8) to ensure that it is not sung too fast. Begin with soloists, perhaps adding an additional instrumental stanza between the second and third stanzas of text (perhaps with clarinet or saxophone).

How lovely, Lord, how lovely (2042)
Theme: The joy of eternal life in God

This hymn is a rendering of Psalm 84 and celebrates the joy of believers in the family of God. It is appropriate in observing eternal life and the nature of God's kingdom, particularly for funeral or memorial services or for All Saints. The first half of stanza 1 could be used as a musical response for the Psalter setting in *The United Methodist Hymnal* (page 804).

The melody is easy to sing and remember, and its use of the same notes and rhythm for three of its four phrases makes it especially usable with young children. This text, with its use of references to abiding place, sparrows finding shelter and a nesting place, God as sun and shield, and showers of blessing, provides a good source of teaching for young people about the nature of God.

How Majestic Is Your Name (2023)
See "O Lord, our Lord, how majestic is your name."

Humble thyself in the sight of the Lord (2131)
Themes: Grace; humility; redemption

This song calls the congregation to an attitude of humility before God. Accordingly, it would be a good call to prayer. In services with prayers of confession, especially services of Holy Communion, this song would work well immediately before the confession. It would also effectively lead into a congregational psalm of confession, such as Psalm 51 (UMH, 785).

This song should be sung rather slowly, about 64 beats per minute, with simple accompaniment. The first lyrical phrase ("Humble thyself in the sight of the Lord") should be sung and played softly, while the second phrase ("and he shall lift you up") should be sung and played more strongly. The song could be sung in unison, with everyone singing part 1; or it could be sung as a call and response, with a soloist singing part 1 and the congregation singing part 2. Other combinations of parts 1 and 2 may be used (right side/left side, men/women, and so on).

I am weak, but thou art strong (2158)
Themes: Strength in tribulation; personal holiness; spiritual formation

This is a fervent prayer to a Jesus who is strong when I am weak, who cares and shares my burdens when no one else does, who will guide me even through the passage of death. It is a cry for help going beyond "talking the talk" to "walking the walk." As part of an opening praise service or medley of praise choruses, it is an eloquent invocation. As a response to preaching, it is not an act of commitment in our own strength but a petition for the help without which no commitment or growth is possible. This song is effectively sung in a wide variety of styles. The accompaniment should be sensitive to the people's stylistic intuitions and be respectful of the song's emotional intensity.

Given the origins of this song in the early years of jazz and frequent setting by Dixieland groups at funerals and wakes especially in the southern USA, it would be appropriate to introduce or conclude the singing of this hymn with an accompanied solo trumpet, and for the soloist to add a judicious amount of stylistic elaboration of the tune.

I am your mother (2059)
(Earth Prayer)
Themes: Thanksgiving for Creation; nature; sin; living in community; communion with the earth

This hymn is a strong prayer for forgiveness of our treatment of the earth, matched by a strong tune. It might be introduced as a prayer reading by three voices, with all joining on the final stanza or as solo stanzas. It is appropriate for the Sunday nearest Earth Day, in conjunction with Creation stories in Genesis and John, at Thanksgiving, on Ash Wednesday or other times of confession.

The tune may be introduced with instruments (e.g., clarinet) or in octaves on the keyboard. For all of its jumps, it is a compelling tune, and after the congregation has had a chance to hear it several times, they will want to join in. Use it as a call to prayer, a prayer of confession, as meditation before a related sermon, at church camps and retreats.

I cast all my cares upon you (2215)
Themes: Comfort and encouragement; faith and hope; God's guidance and care; trust

The text for this chorus is taken from Psalm 55:22 and 1 Peter 5:7 and could be sung anytime these scriptures are used in worship. Incorporate "Cares Chorus" into a medley of songs related to the theme of prayer. Read the passages from

Psalms and 1 Peter and sing the chorus together. Then invite the congregation to offer prayers silently or aloud. End the time of prayer by singing the chorus together once again. This chorus would also be very appropriate to use in services of healing and wholeness.

I have decided to follow Jesus (2129)
Themes: Invitation to discipleship and our response; commitment; the Cross
This simple hymn is appropriate for times of commitment and in the midst of struggles. It might be used at the beginning of worship to remind us of our commitment, or after the sermon in response to the inviting Word. It could also be sung during an altar call. When a church or community is in the midst of struggles, the third stanza might be adapted to fit the situation, for example: "Though floods are raging, still I will follow. . . . In times of trial, still I will follow. . . . In times of crisis, God will go with us."
Simple accompaniments or *a cappella* voices are most appropriate for this hymn. Let it arise from the congregation, and grow in strength. Change "I" to "we" in times of solidarity.

I have found a friend in Jesus (2062)
Themes: Praise of Jesus Christ; God's providential care; thanksgiving
This acclamation of joy in Jesus our friend, with opening imagery from the Song of Solomon, may appeal to persons who find picturing Jesus as King or even Lord distancing and unappealing. It can appropriately follow preaching that pictures Jesus as our friend. It fits well in services with an evangelistic emphasis, where it can be sung by a soloist or congregation as a testimony or be a fitting congregational response to someone's personal testimony. It can be used in an opening praise service. It may be especially effective with older persons who remember this song from their youth, in reawakening their old faith and fervor. It should be sung and accompanied in a lively, rollicking way that brings out its bubbling joy.
Variety can be attained by having the women's voices of the choir sing the tenor part an octave higher on one or more stanzas, resulting in a descant.

I love you, Lord (2068)
Themes: Adoration and praise; God's grace; our love for Jesus Christ
This popular chorus is a beautiful setting of several psalms and 2 Chronicles 6:40. It is usually considered a prayer song but would fit well at any point in a worship service. It is especially meaningful to have a soloist, who is not seen by the congregation, sing it *a cappella* before the prayer. Also, have a worship leader read 2 Chronicles 6:40 before it is sung.
Use it in a medley of songs to lead the congregation into a quiet time of worship. Some possible companion songs are "My Jesus, I Love Thee" (UMH,

172) and "Father, I Adore You" (2038). If this song is used by itself, consider adding a modulation to G major for the final time and using sign language for a beautiful visual interpretation.

I sing praises to your name (2037)
Themes: Praise; adoration

This song may be used in a variety of worship styles. It may be included in a praise medley, or during a time of prayer. Play the accompaniment as the worship leader prays on behalf of the congregation. Have the music continue as people are encouraged to pray silently. Congregations can sing this song during communion, or during other worship rituals, such as anointing with oil. It can be used as an invitation to worship, or as an introduction to and/or response to the scripture reading. Consider changing the "I" to "we" for a more corporate statement of worship.

I sought him dressed in finest clothes (2094)
Themes: Epiphany; coming of the Magi; justice

"Carol of the Epiphany" recalls the surprise that the Magi must have felt when they found the baby Jesus. Though it may be sung by a congregation, it is most effective when sung by three soloists. Use it following the Matthew 2:1-12 reading on Epiphany Sunday.

The three soloists may begin in three different locations in the worship space, moving to a central point by the end of stanza 4. Perhaps a manger or crèche that was used during the Christmas season could be placed where the soloists gather at the end of the song. It will be much more effective if the soloists memorize their stanzas and deliver them very dramatically. If you do not plan for the congregation to join on stanza 5, consider a dramatic slowing of the tempo in the last two sung measures, "We touched God in a baby's hand."

I was there to hear your borning cry (2051)
Themes: God's care; birth; baptism; confirmation; marriage; death

This incredibly sensitive song has become very popular in recent years. Though never stated, the "I" of the text is God. Notice the "if" of stanza 4 when referring to marriage and the sensitive way the end of stanza 4 makes God a part of all love, including physical love.

This song is very appropriate for worship that celebrates young persons: baptism, confirmation, graduation, and so on. It makes an excellent introduction or response to these special observances. The melody is quickly learned and can be sung easily by a congregation. It might be best introduced by a soloist singing stanzas 1-6 with the congregation joining on stanza 7. But after a couple of hearings, the congregation will want to join in. The best accompaniment is simple, using either guitar or piano. Avoid an excessively dramatic treatment and let the text and tune speak for themselves.

I will call upon the Lord (2002)
Themes: Praise and adoration of God; deliverance

This energetic song based on Psalm 18 works well any time of the year as a song of praise or a call to worship. Initially, a song leader or other small ensemble should sing part 1. The congregation sings part 2, echoing the leader's part. After the song is learned, other combinations of groups may be designated as part1/part 2 (men/women; right side/left side). The refrain is printed in unison for the congregation but works well when the alto, tenor, and bass harmonization is added by a praise team or choir (parts included in the Accompaniment and Singer's Editions).

As the tempo of this song should be with a lively bounce ($\downarrow$ = 116), its style is most appropriate as an opening for worship. Create an opening medley by including some of the following: "He Is Exalted" (2070); "Praise the Name of Jesus" (2066); or "Holy, Holy, Holy! Lord God Almighty" (UMH, 64).

I will come to you in the silence (2218)
Themes: God's care; strength; baptism

God calls; we respond. "You Are Mine" is a reminder that no matter where we are and how low we may feel, God is always there, calling to us, and inviting us to follow. This song can be very inspirational, especially as it allows us to hear God speaking directly to us. Note that all of the text is written from God's perspective. Use it during Lent to remind us that God is with us as we approach Good Friday. Use it in the weeks following Easter when the scriptures tell of Jesus appearing to the apostles and giving them the Holy Spirit.

Introduce the refrain by using it alone with prayers of petition. You might do this for several weeks. When the congregation is familiar with the refrain, sing the entire song with a soloist or a duet singing the stanzas. Add the refrain optional harmony after stanza 3. Repeat the refrain twice after stanza 4. Accompany with piano, guitar, and bass.

I will enter his gates (2270)
Themes: Adoration; thanksgiving and praise

This popular praise song overflows with joy and triumph. The composer has said that this song was God's way of teaching her that thanksgiving is the key to experiencing the joy of the Lord. Because it contains the Bible's pattern for worship, "Enter his gates with thanksgiving, and his courts with praise," it is ideal for the opening of a worship service. Worship should be a journey moving each one to God's presence. It is the thanksgiving and praise that brings us into that place where we truly worship our God.

The worship leader might read a few scriptures about entering into worship before the song begins or while the introduction is being played. A medley of songs that exemplifies this pattern (thanksgiving, praise, worship) would include: "We Bring the Sacrifice of Praise" (2031) and "Surely the Presence of the Lord" (UMH, 328).

If it had not been for the Lord (2053)
Themes: Trust and assurance of the love of God; confidence based on experience and prayer

This song is a personal and communal testimony of ways that God intercedes in moments of human trials and conflicts. The text should be sung slowly in order to express the deeply emotional feeling that the song conveys. Care should be taken to maintain the slow and steady harmonic progressions of the accompaniment, which helps to establish and maintain the spiritual depth intended by the composer. The opening refrain is structured so that it can be easily learned by the congregation, first in unison, and then with the addition of the harmony. Different soloists should sing the verses initially. Once the melodic lines of the verses are learned, the community should be encouraged to sing with the soloists.

This song can be used effectively as a prayer response, an act of praise, or following the words of assurance.

I'll Fly Away (2282)
See "Some glad morning."

I'm gonna live so God can use me (2153)
Themes: Affirmation of commitment and rededication; rebirth

This spiritual can be used as a response to numerous calls to commitment in an order of service, such as words of assurance, response to the Word (sermon), or invitation to discipleship. It can also serve as the congregation's affirmation to God's call to service in the world.

Due to the simplicity of this spiritual it can be taught during worship. Children's choirs can easily help lead this song.

I'm so glad Jesus lifted me (2151)
Themes: Thankful response for a religious experience; conversion and rebirth; freedom

This exuberant testimony of freedom is the result of a religious encounter and a lifting of burdens. It evokes the feeling of newness of life for individuals and communities of faith. The personal pronouns used in the text are deliberate, but are also effective as a communal testimony merging individual spiritual encounters as a total offering of thanksgiving to God in Jesus the Christ. When understood in light of its origin in the African American slave community, this spiritual can be interpreted as an anticipation of freedom, and a coded message for slaves to meet at the entrance of the Underground Railroad in order to be lifted into freedom land.

In the liturgy this spiritual is an appropriate response between the confession and words of assurance, following the pastoral prayer, and following a service of healing. Its repetitive style, structured in short, syncopated phrases, makes it possible to modulate a half step higher at each verse. This movement breaks the monotony of repetition, adds momentum to congregational singing, and helps convey the feeling of being lifted from one level of spiritual existence to another.

In his time (2203)

Themes: God's guidance and care; faith and hope; our response to God

Ecclesiastes 3:11 is beautifully set to music with this simple melody. It should be sung with a moderate flowing tempo ($\downarrow$ = 84-92). The reverent style suggests its use during a time of prayer or a quiet worship medley. It could also be used during a time of sharing by the congregation. Intersperse the singing of the chorus with witnesses about how God has made things beautiful in each person's life, or have a small ensemble sing it while the congregation reflects on their personal response to God's guidance and care.

Congregations concerned with inclusive language may choose to sing "in your time" throughout the song. This change also makes the whole song addressed to God rather than switching from speaking about God to speaking to God as the original text suggests.

In our lives, Lord, be glorified (2150)

Themes: Commitment; service; ministry in daily life

This popular prayer chorus is particularly appropriate as a response to the Word. It can easily be used as a song of commitment or a song to send the people out in ministry in the world. Because the text is simple and repetitive, worship leaders may add more verses by substituting other words in place of "lives" that reflect the theme of the worship service, such as "work," "songs," or "worship."

This song may also be used as a musical frame for prayers of intercession. Between each verse, as the instrumental accompaniment continues, the worship leader invites the congregation to offer prayers silently or aloud. The leader may wish to prompt particular prayers by saying, "Together let us pray for," filling in appropriate areas of concern, including those who suffer, communities and congregations, the world, and the church universal.

In remembrance of me (2254)
Theme: Holy Communion

This popular communion anthem by Buryl Red and Ragan Courtney has been sung by many choirs since its first appearance in 1972. As a result, congregations have become familiar with the melody and will find this setting accessible with some direction by the song leader. The arrangement may seem confusing and even overwhelming at first. However, the melody and text flow naturally to such a degree that most congregations will be able to sing the whole arrangement after a short rehearsal prior to the service or at another appropriate gathering in the church life, such as a Sunday school assembly, social gathering, or church dinners.

This song would also be appropriate on Maundy Thursday as the Last Supper is reenacted.

In the Lord I'll be ever thankful (2195)
Themes: Thanksgiving; assurance; hope

This lively selection comes from the Taizé Community, an ecumenical monastic group in southeastern France. It is sung as a part of their prayer services, which meet three times each day. This song should be sung at a lively tempo with confidence. Do not let it drag. Parts for flute, oboe, trumpet, and other instruments can be found in the Accompaniment Edition. Sing several times (at least three) in order to securely establish the mood and give the congregation an opportunity to enjoy this playful, folklike melody. Introduce with a flute followed by a solo voice. Add harmony with the choir and other instrumental parts as it is repeated.

This song can be used as a response to prayers of thanksgiving or as a psalm response for any psalms with themes of gratitude, assurance, or hope.

In the midst of new dimensions (2238)
Themes: The nature of the church; hope in the future; hope in the midst of a change; community; faith; trust; cultural diversity

This hymn is concerned with instilling hope in the future amidst a changing world order. Subtle language refutes dire apocalyptic predictions and encourages faith, not fear of the future. Despite the appearance that the world seems divided, the hymn emphasizes the commonality of all people: "We, your global village, might envision wider dreams."

The tune and setting have a festive character that would make the hymn well suited as a concluding hymn in a service concerned with hope in the future. The refrain is strong enough to stand on its own as a separate chorus.

In the singing, in the silence (2255)
Themes: Holy Communion; the grace and peace of Jesus Christ; blessing; healing

This hymn for communion is rich with images as we come together to receive Christ's grace and peace at the table. Here all the tensions of life are held in God's hands: singing/silence, blessing/breaking, question/answer, and heart's cry/healing. With its varied images and lovely music this hymn is destined to become a favorite of congregations.

Begin with soloists on the stanzas and let everyone join on the refrain. The melody is simple enough that even beginning instrumentalists might play it. (Use an easier key for beginners and have them play during the prelude or offertory.) Sing it before communion and during the distribution. Then let the congregation learn the stanzas, so that this may be a song sung from the heart during the distribution as Christ meets us at the Table.

In unity we lift our song (2221)

Themes: Community of faith; heritage and tradition; scripture; biblical narrative; Mother's Day; Father's Day; church anniversaries; dedication of a building; memorial services; funeral services

This hymn by Ken Medema is set to Martin Luther's familiar tune, EIN' FESTE BURG ("A Mighty Fortress Is Our God"). The stateliness of the music adds a dignity that complements the strength of the text. Together they create a new hymn that has the potential to become a standard for congregations that may rival the original Martin Luther text. Medema's hymn is rich in metaphors for areas where there seems to be a shortage of good hymns: the Bible (biblical narrative), stories and traditions, hope in times of despair, hope in facing death. Consequently, this hymn would be particularly well suited for a service that honors the faith, contributions, and heritage of older members of a congregation. Their stories, personal strength, nurturing and faithfulness have set examples for all members of the church community.

Because of its strength and dignity, the hymn would be well suited for opening or closing a service. The descant sung by high voices in the choir would add a high level of energy and enthusiasm. If the descant is used, the final stanza should be sung in unison. One possibility would be to have the first stanza in unison, second stanza women only, third stanza men only, final stanza all with choir descant. This would also be an opportunity for an optional, more florid accompaniment, such as that found in *The United Methodist Hymnal: Music Supplement* (#113). For a greater challenge and rhythmic interest, consider using the arrangement based on the original tune (#111). If this proves to be too challenging for the congregation, one stanza of the hymn could be sung by the choir using this arrangement.

Into my heart (2160)

Themes: Personal holiness; commitment

This simple prayer to Jesus is readily memorized and has a variety of uses. Early in worship, by itself or as part of a medley of praise choruses, it is a heartfelt invocation. The first stanza can serve as a call to prayer. After preaching, it can be a prayer for the ever-present help that alone make commitment possible. Whenever sung, it may be followed by a time of silent reflection. It is an effective communion song when many persons are standing or kneeling and unable to use a hymnal or look at a screen. Where no accompaniment is available, it is easily and effectively sung without accompaniment.

A small choir can easily adapt the tenor line to go with the soprano line as a two-part choral arrangement. For one stanza have women sing the melody and men sing the tenor part. For stanza 2 have men sing the melody and women sing the tenor line an octave higher.

It is the cry of my heart (2165)
Themes: Commitment; personal holiness

"Cry of My Heart" is a beautiful prayer that would be appropriate to be sung both before the sermon and as a response to the sermon. Use this song as a sung prayer for illumination before the scriptures are read or prior to the sermon. Have the congregation sing the refrain and a soloist sing the verses. Following the sermon, have the congregation sing it as a prayer of commitment. Accompaniment may be supplied by organ or piano but it would also be very effective accompanied with only an acoustic guitar.

I've got peace like a river (2145)
Themes: Assurance; peace; love; joy

This African American spiritual is very popular with children. Some members may remember this song from their camping days. It makes a wonderful song for children to share in worship, adding sign language on the words peace, joy, love, river, fountain, ocean, and soul. Use this song as part of an opening praise medley that speaks of our joy as we gather for worship.

It also works well as a response to the Word, especially when the Word proclaimed speaks of the fruits that come from the spiritual life in contrast to earthly rewards. Scriptures that speak of the depth of God's love for us and the peace and joy that come from being in relationship with Christ, are enhanced by this upbeat spiritual.

I've just come from the fountain (2250)
Themes: Baptism; reaffirmation; renewal

A fresh dip in the fountain is renewing and transforming. This spiritual will add vitality to any congregation in its placement immediately following baptism and congregational reaffirmation of the baptismal covenant. The melody should be introduced prior to the service so that its inclusion will flow without interruption. Use the choir to introduce this song, then invite the congregation to join in.

Jesu, Tawa Pano **(2273)**
See "Jesus, we are here."

Jesus Be Praised **(2079)**
See "Jesus, we worship you."

Jesus, draw me close (2159)
Themes: Praise; worship; the name of Jesus

This praise chorus would work well at the end of an opening praise medley. It invites Jesus to be present in the worship time and is a nice, slow meditative song to bring people deeper into a place of the spirit and readiness to be open to God's direction. It also works well sung by itself. This song is appropriate in a time of confession, because the text states the desire to "worship and obey." Follow this song with scripture, and then sing the song again after the scripture reading. If you do the song a few times in a row, consider modulating the song to G major. Sing it two more times, dropping the accompaniment except for light percussion. You may also wish to consider using the pronouns "we" and "our," instead of "me" and "my."

Jesus, name above all names (2071)
Themes: Praise; worship; the name of Jesus

Philippians 2:9 tells us that God has given his Son, Jesus, a name that is highly exalted above every other name. Naida Hearn has set this thought in a simple chorus that would be appropriate to sing in any service of praise. Use this as a medley with the hymn "Fairest Lord Jesus" (UMH, 189). Be sure to sing the fourth stanza written by Joseph A. Seiss: "Beautiful Savior! Lord of all the nations!" Maintain the flowing 12/8 meter throughout the medley. You might also want to prepare a responsive reading of scriptures dealing with the different names given to Jesus. Intersperse these readings between the chorus and hymn stanzas.

This song is also especially appropriate to use with children.

Jesus rode into Jerusalem (2109)
Theme: Palm Sunday

This Palm Sunday song was written to be an entrance for children and others who process in the worship service. Have children carry palm branches with them as the song is sung. You may wish to dramatize the entrance by having someone portraying Jesus also enter with the children. Introduce this before it is sung by having the music play as the worship leader tells people what it was like in Jerusalem the day Jesus came to town. Explain that the word Hosanna means "save us now."

Do this song with a lead singer, and have the congregation sing the "Hosanna! Hosanna!" response and the refrain. This frees the congregation to watch the processional as they sing. Experiment with rhythms and percussion instruments to make this tune rock!

Jesus, tempted in the desert (2105)
Themes: Jesus' life; temptation

This vivid retelling of Jesus' temptation as he began his ministry is a reminder that we, too, are tempted. It is very appropriate on the first Sunday in Lent or in any worship that addresses the power God gives us to do what is right. Stanza 4 becomes more appropriate if used on a Sunday when communion is celebrated.

Use this hymn as a frame for the lectionary Gospel reading of the temptation story. Using three readers, have oen read the verses about the firs temptation. Sing the first verse. The second reader shares the verses about the second temptation, followed by the second verse. The third temptation and verse are treated in the same manner. The fourth verse may follow the sermon as a response to the Word. In Year A, when the Matthew version of trhe text is read, sing the verses of the hymn in order. In Year C, when the Luke version is read, sing verse 3 before verse 2 to match the order of the scripture text.

The text can be introduced as a spoken reading. Three readers (a narrator, Jesus, Satan) can easily divide the text and proclaim it in a dramatic fashion. Dancers might also be used to enhance the presentation. When sung, the tempo should move along ($\downarrow$ = 76-88). It is a long hymn and some singers can tire of it. Ask the choir to sing stanza 1, the right half of the congregation to sing stanza 2, and the left half to sing stanza 3. All may join together on stanza 4. This engages the singer's interest and heightens the concept of the three temptations.

Jesus walked this lonesome valley (2112)
Themes: Christ's Passion; personal commitment to Christ

This familiar folk hymn is especially fitting for Holy Week and Good Friday, but perhaps also at those times when we feel alone, isolated, or endure trials privately. This text seems to conflict with the promise of Psalm 23, which claims God's presence in such moments and times, yet Christians all experience, as did Jesus, occasions of isolation, even forsakenness.

A steady, slow tempo, unchanging rhythm, and quiet volume will contribute to the appropriate, somber mood of this hymn. The melody can be sung or played canonically (as a round), which might be quite appropriate for stanza 2. A second voice, choir section, or instrument can enter after the first four beats, as the word *walked* is being sustained by the first voice. It is more of an echo effect than a canon, especially if the second voice is quieter than the first.

Jesus, we are here (2273)
Jesu, Tawa Pano
Themes: Gathering; assurance; entrance into worship; praise

This is a classic processional song in the Shona language of Zimbabwe, used to gather the people for worship. It was written by United Methodist church musician Patrick Matsikenyiri, who teaches at Africa University in Mutare, Zimbabwe. It is accompanied usually only by a hosho (a maraca-type shaker with seeds inside) playing eighth-note patterns. A light drum is possible, but not necessary. A simple swaying is also part of the response to the song. Invite the choir to glide between the two chords each time "Jesu" or "Jesus" is sung. The leader can indicate word changes for the following stanzas by singing them over the final half note: "Welcome, Savior"; "Welcome, Master"; "Welcome, Spirit"; and so on. By doing this, the people will soon be able to free themselves from their books and join in the singing and swaying. Remember that the word for *music* in most African languages means singing, dancing, and playing instruments all at once.

Tawa pano ("we are here") is an important phrase that signifies community in the Shona church. The song should be sung several times until those who have gathered individually feel as one body in Christ. This song may be sung on any Sunday as a part of the gathering. It might also be sung as a preparation for prayer. Sing it unaccompanied if at all possible and maintain a steady beat until the final cadence. It is appropriate for the soloist to improvise a part every two measures over the ends of the phrases, leading into the next measure. The final measure has an example of this, but the soloist is not limited to this measure.

Jesus, we worship you (2079)
Themes: Adoration; praise

"Jesus Be Praised" is a simple, yet beautiful declaration of praise and worship to Jesus Christ. This chorus would be very effective in a quiet, reflective time of worship. You might want to begin the service by having the choir process down two aisles singing this song as a canon. One side of the choir would start singing alone and the second group would begin singing four measures later. Begin singing *a cappella* and have the organ, piano or keyboard, or guitar enter after the round has been sung two times. Sing through the chorus once more and then invite the congregation to join the choir. This chorus would also work well in a medley of hymns in praise of Christ.

Joseph dearest, Joseph mine (2099)
Theme: Christmas

These lyrics were originally sung as a lullaby by the Virgin Mary in sixteenth-century mystery plays in Leipzig, Germany. Ralph Vaughan Williams's setting is suitable for any Christmas service and should be sung by the congregation in unison, with the refrain in parts if possible. The lilting 6/8 rhythm creates a lullaby feel by its gentle pulses on beats 1 and 4. Consequently, the hymn should definitely not be rushed but should be sung in a tempo that would naturally imitate the swaying motion of a mother rocking a baby.

Since the text is organized in a dialogue style as a conversation between Mary and Joseph, one format for singing would be for all the women to sing the first stanza, all the men sing the second stanza, then everyone sing the final stanza. The refrain could be sung by everyone at the end of each stanza. Another option would be to let children or a children's choir sing the refrain, with everyone singing the final refrain. The phrase, "Jesus, Jesus" toward the end of the refrain could be sung very softly in keeping with the spirit of a lullaby.

Joy comes with the dawn (2210)
Themes: Joy; grace; strength in tribulation; resurrection; rejoicing after sorrow

This song reminds the congregation of God's grace, which is new every morning bringing joy with the dawn (Lam. 3:22-23). It would function well as an anthem by a choir or ensemble or as a congregational song with a few choir members singing the optional descant. As another option, a flute or other solo instrument could play the descant part.

This song might be particularly effective during a communion service, a worship service soon after Easter, a service of morning praise and prayer, or in a memorial service, reminding the congregation of our hope in the resurrection to come. The tempo should be about 80 beats per minute.

Joy in the Morning (2284)
See "There'll be joy in the morning."

Joys are flowing like a river (2142)
Themes: Transforming power of the Holy Spirit; strength in tribulation

An excellent reminder of the calming power of the Holy Spirit, this hymn can be effectively performed at either a slow or upbeat pace. It is appropriate during Pentecost Sunday or during the time after Pentecost in several places in the worship service, such as the words of assurance or prayer for illumination. The refrain is also appropriate as a sung response to Matthew 8:23-27; Mark 4:35-41; and Luke 8:22-25. It would also be a fitting song to use in a morning or evening prayer service for centering.

Jubilate Servite (2017)
See "Come, rejoice in God."

Just a Closer Walk with Thee **(2158)**
See "I am weak, but thou art strong."

King of kings and Lord of lords (2075)
Themes: Names for Jesus; praise
    This lively song would be a great opening song or closing song to follow a dismissal with a blessing. Use this song in a medley with other songs that praise the various names that we use for Jesus Christ.
    Start the song slowly and gradually get faster. Also, begin with simple instrumentation and increase the intensity as the song develops. Include hand claps on each rest after the word *glory* is sung. Sing it in canon with the second part entering when the first part sings "Jesus, Prince of peace." An Israeli-style dance would also be fun to use with this song.

Kyrie **(2127)**
See "Come and see."

Kyrie (2275)
Themes: Mercy; prayers of intercession
    When the language of worship shifted from Greek to Latin, this prayer remained in Greek, and it continues to be a powerful reminder of our connection with the communion of the saints through the ages to sing it that way in the twenty-first century. "Lord, have mercy; Christ, have mercy; Lord, have mercy," we pray. This cry for mercy is not restricted to God's forgiving grace, but includes the "manifold blessings" we seek in so many ways.
    Ruth Elaine Schram has taken that historic prayer and set it to the haunting melody often known as "Going Home" from Dvořák's *New World* Symphony. Each phrase can begin softly, grow in intensity, and then ease up. In the final phrase, the second "Kyrie" builds to a peak of intensity and volume on the E, then decrescendos, with the final "eleison" sung very softly. The words are pronounced "Kee-ree-aye," "Chrees-taye," and "aye-lay-ee-zohn."
    Because many in the congregation may already be familiar with the melody, introduce the song by simply stating the text at the beginning of each section. Include a note in the worship order with the translation or share it aloud prior to singing.

Lamb of God **(2113)**
See "Your only Son."

Lead me, guide me (2214)
Themes: Confession; prayer for strength in tribulation

The refrain of this gospel song can be used effectively as the opening statement of the prayer of confession, followed by a verbal prayer. It may also serve as a transitional statement between the confession and the words of assurance. It is also effective as one of the songs during Ash Wednesday. With its lilting melody, congregations have no difficulty learning this song with the assistance of the choir or song leading team.

Lead on, O cloud of Presence (2234)
Themes: The presence of God; freedom and liberation; hope

Built on the Exodus imagery of Numbers 9:15-23, this text uses the tune and focus of "Lead On, O King Eternal" without its emphasis on militaristic triumphalism. The widely quoted last phrase of stanza 2 ("The journey is our home") is a summary of Ruth Duck's theme in this hymn: the presence of God guiding us and giving us hope even when we are beset by uncertainty.

This hymn works well as a processional hymn, although it is also effective as a hymn of mission or going forth at the end of a service. There are a number of arrangements of the tune LANCASHIRE for organ and/or brass that can be used. The tempo should give the feeling of a steady and persistent movement forward, avoiding the tendency of many congregations to sing more and more slowly.

Let all things now living (2008)
Themes: God's praise in Creation; thanksgiving

Many will recall this joyous tune from their youthful summer camp experiences. This hymn is best presented in that same exuberant spirit. The dance-like mood could be established by a solo flute or trumpet as an introduction or interlude between stanzas. The keyboard accompanist can contribute to this spirit with a light registration and a detached style. Organists might consider an extended dominant C pedal point during the third of the hymn's four phrases to add contrast and build tension.

The opening phrase of stanza 1 can be used as another response for Psalm 150 (UMH, 862), and it would be appropriate to then sing the entire hymn following the psalm. Consider having children's choirs add instruments of various kinds following selected verses of the psalm. The text of the hymn is rich with images to inspire liturgical dancers, including the use of banners and candles or other lights.

Let us be bread (2260)
Themes: Holy Communion; discipleship; commitment; service to the world

This song is a prayer for us to be the bread of life to the world, in the name of Jesus. Sing the refrain twice through before going to the verses. Have the choir, vocal team, or a soloist sing the verses. Consider singing the first and second verses together, before returning to the refrain. Sing the refrain, verse 3; refrain, verse 4; then the refrain twice. Alternately, you may skip the refrain between verses 3 and 4. Add the descant on all refrains after verse 3.

Sing this song as a preparation for communion. Play the tune through communion for a more meditative experience.

Let us offer to the Father (2262)
Te Ofrecemos Padre Nuestro
Themes: Holy Communion; commitment; daily living

This lively song from the Nicaraguan Mass reminds the community of faith that it must bring to God not only the gifts of bread and wine (gifts from our hand), but also gifts from the heart, from our whole being.

The tune invites the congregation to dance. The leader could encourage this by doing a slight swaying motion to the right and left, as he or she leads the song, indicating that the gift of movement or motion is one we also offer to God. Another rhythm possibility is to have one small group clapping hands while the rest of the congregation sings. Clapping could be in the following manner:

Finger cymbals and claves could be added to the hand clapping, on beats 1 and 4:

This communion song can be used while the elements are being brought forward. It is very effective when the persons bringing the elements to the front use the swaying motion mentioned above, swinging the arms in a slow, rocking motion first to the right, then to the left:

> Measure 1: First step, right foot, swing arms slowly to the right in upward motion.
> Measure 2: Second step, left foot, swing arms slowly to the left in upward motion, and so on.

This song is also appropriate for Worldwide Communion Sunday. Guitar or piano accompaniment is suitable. Suggested tempo: ($\bullet$ = 66).

Let us with a joyful mind (2012)

Themes: The glory of God; praise to God; the beauty of God's Creation

This hymn is an adaptation of John Milton's text, "Let us with gladsome mind," based on Psalm 136. The melody of the verse and refrain are the same. Consequently, the hymn will be easy to learn for congregations who are unfamiliar with the tune.

Although the hymn is not an exact paraphrase of Psalm 136, it does parallel individual verses of the psalm. One effective way to use the hymn would be to alternate reading individual psalm verses with the singing of their respective hymn stanzas. For example, Psalm 136: read verse 1, sing stanza 1; read verse 7, sing stanza 2; read verse 8, sing stanza 3; read verse 9, sing stanza 4.

Thomas Troeger's adaptation is reminiscent of #92 ("For the Beauty of the Earth") and #147 ("All Things Bright and Beautiful") in *The United Methodist Hymnal*. These hymns give praise for various aspects of God's Creation: the earth, the sky, stars, the ocean, creatures, and so forth. It would be interesting to use these three hymns as a hymn medley in a service based on the theme of God's Creation.

Life-giving bread (2261)

Themes: Holy Communion; transformation and new life; redemption; service; witness

In this song we quietly celebrate Christ's sacramental gift of himself to and for us. A soloist or ensemble should first teach the refrain to the congregation. After this, everyone could sing the refrain, with the soloist or group singing each stanza. The last time through the refrain, a few high voices could sing the optional descant. If preferred, a flute or other solo instrument could play the descant instead.

Piano alone would provide suitable accompaniment, as would guitar. If two or more instruments provide the accompaniment, only one should play the arpeggiated accompaniment. The other instrument(s) should play sustained chords, making for an uncluttered sound. If organ is used, it should play the sustained notes in the bass clef of the accompaniment; the right hand should simply support the voice parts. The tempo should be approximately 102-106 beats per minute.

Light of the World (2204)

See "You are the Light of the World."

Light the Advent candle (2090)

Themes: Children and lighting the candles in the Advent wreath

Themes for the four Sundays in Advent can be found in key words in the four stanzas: waiting, wonder, peace, joy. Be alert: if the congregation follows the practice of having the third candle be a different color (pink) on "joy

Sunday," it will be difficult to make this song fit. Stanzas 3 and 4 cannot simply be exchanged because of the rhyme of "four" with "forevermore." If you want the refrain to include an Advent prayer, the last half of the refrain can be altered to read: "Come, Christ Jesus, come to stay; fill us with your light today."

Avoid singing and playing this song as if it were a waltz. Instead of a heavy stress on beats 1 and 2 with a very light third beat, think of the tempo as *legato*, with one beat to the measure.

Like a child (2092)
Themes: Advent; Jesus' life and teaching; children

Jesus' birth as a child and his acceptance of the children around him in the Gospels of Matthew, Mark, and Luke are the major themes of this hymn. It may be used in the Advent, Christmas, and Epiphany seasons or when these Gospel lessons appear in the lectionary. It would also be appropriate on the national observance of Children's Sabbaths, an ecumenical observance in October of each year. See http://www.childrensdefense.org/sabbath.html for more information.

Accompany this hymn on piano or guitar. The tempo should be gentle ($\downarrow$ = 80). The flute descant would also be nice played on a recorder (small flute-like instrument that many children learn to play in elementary school). Use the recorder or flute to introduce the melody in the introduction as well. A child soloist might also be used to teach the melody to the congregation.

Live in charity (2179)
Ubi Caritas
Themes: Christian unity; reconciliation; love of God; assurance

This song is perhaps the most widely known contribution of the Taizé Community, an ecumenical monastic movement that began during World War II in occupied France. In many ways it captures the primary themes of Taizé—reconciliation and peace among all. Singing it in Latin reminds one of the original Latin poem from which the text comes and establishes a link with Christians who have prayed this prayer for well over one thousand years. Sing as a benediction, preparation for prayer, during communion, for a wedding, during a service of foot washing, or any other occasion when reconciliation is an important theme.

This song can be sung in several ways. The Accompaniment Edition provides several instrumental suggestions. Also included are song leader's parts that allows one to sing scripture above the second half of the melody. There is also a chanted version of 1 Corinthians 13 that may be sung by a choir or soloist. In this case, "Ubi caritas" becomes a response that is sung at various points throughout the chanting of this passage rather than a repeated ostinato chorus.

Living for Jesus (2149)
Themes: Personal commitment in daily living; sending forth

This is a song of response to the gospel of God's grace in Christ. The author, an ordained Methodist clergyman, also wrote "Great Is Thy Faithfulness." It is fitting after preaching that lifts up God's grace as calling for the response of a changed daily life. It is a song for times of sending forth to life in the world. It is a pledge of allegiance to the Guide we need in all our daily decisions.

While its tempo is not fast, it is important not to let it drag or become schmaltzy. The unrelenting rhythmic pattern of quarter–half–quarter in every measure of the verse can easily cause a congregation to drag the tempo ever slower with each verse. The tempo does not have to be quick, but the accompanist playing in a strong feel of cut time will help prevent this dragging. It should be firm and strong, as befits the message.

Lord, Be Glorified (2150)
See "In our lives, Lord, be glorified."

Lord God, Almighty (2006)
Themes: Praise and thanksgiving; worship; Trinity

This simple statement of praise and thanksgiving could be effectively used as a response to the Word. It might also be used to frame prayers of praise and joy. Sing the chorus through and then invite the congregation to offer prayers silently or aloud, acknowledging God's attributes. The second stanza mentions each person of the Trinity. It would be appropriate to use this stanza as a doxological response after the offering.

The verse in which God speaks would be appropriately sung by a soloist. The second verse may also be sung by a soloist or by the whole congregation. Although the rhythms have been altered to accommodate more text, the melody of the verses has the same shape of the chorus and should be easy for the congregation to sing after the chorus is learned.

Lord, have mercy (2277)
Themes: Confession and assurance of pardon

Swee Hong Lim uses the "Kyrie" (see "Kyrie," 2275, for a description) before and after an affirmation of God's forgiving grace in Christ. It may be used as the words of assurance following prayers of confession. The "Lord, have mercy" sections at the beginning and end may be sung by the congregation with a song leader or choir singing the intervening lines.

A sparse and simple accompaniment is recommended. Have a flute or recorder play the melody line, with finger cymbals and/or claves striking softly on the second beat of each measure, or only with the last half note of the longer held notes.

Lord, I lift your name on high (2088)
Themes: Adoration and praise; testimony; statement of faith

One of the most popular of all contemporary songs, "Lord, I lift your name on high" transcends musical style, age, and denominational boundaries. This is a rare gem that can be performed well in any style. It is usually sung at a fairly bright tempo ($\quarternote = 86$).

The text accomplishes something that allows the song to be appropriate at any time of the Christian Year and at any place in the service: it summarizes the whole gospel and responds with adoration.

Use the first two measures, chords only, played two times for the introduction. Repeat the refrain ("You came from heaven to earth") *a cappella* with harmonization by a small ensemble. Then repeat the last phrase ("Lord, I lift your name on high") two times as a closing. A good companion song is "My Life Is in You, Lord" (2032).

Lord, let your kingdom come (2201)
Theme: Intercessory prayer

The spoken text is a bidding prayer (well known from the orders for Morning and Evening Prayer in the UMH). Bonnie Johansen-Werner provides us with music to introduce and to conclude these intercessory prayers. This format can be used at any service.

If your congregation follows the tradition of not singing "Alleluia" during Lent, the "Hear our prayer" of the concluding response may be used as the last measure of the introductory music. The final line with its call and response pattern can also be used as an introduction to the time of prayer and/or after the responses to each bidding (as #485 in *The United Methodist Hymnal* is sometimes used).

Lord, Listen to Your Children (2207)
See "On bended knee."

Lord, listen to your children praying (2193)
Themes: Prayer; love; power; grace; family of God

Like many psalms, this song asks God to hear as God's people pray. Accordingly, it may be used as a musical response to a psalm, such as Psalm 130 (UMH, 848). It could also be used as a response to prayer. Alternatively, it could be sung as a refrain between spoken prayers by the worship leader or by congregation members.

The accompaniment could be very simple, with just a piano or organ. It could also be full, with guitars, keyboards, and percussion. The needs and style of the particular congregation would determine which would be more appropriate. The tempo should be about $\quarternote = 68\text{-}72$ beats per minute.

Lord, may our prayer rise like incense (2205)

Themes: Prayer petitions; thanksgiving

This is a beautiful psalm setting that works especially well with interpretive dance (Pss. 138:1-5; 141:2). Other options would be to use sign language to visually depict the refrain, or have the congregation sign the refrain and dancers interpret the stanzas. You may wish to light a candle on the altar each time the refrain is sung. The visual interpretation will help to keep the melody fresh and lyrical rather than becoming too repetitive.

Have a solo flute or oboe play the refrain as the introduction. During the refrains between the stanzas, a worship leader or pastor could give verbal thanks and praises while the music is sung or played very softly. The refrain can continue to be repeated until the spoken prayers are completed. Keep the melody moving forward ($\downarrow$ = 56-60) in a very *legato* style.

This song is very appropriate during Evening Praise and Prayer after the evening hymn. Light some incense as the scripture text is spoken and follow with the song. As the verses are sung, invite the congregation to come forward and place pieces of incense on the coals as signs of their specific prayer concerns. When using incense in a service, alert those in the congregation who may be sensitive to strong fragrances.

Lord of all hopefulness (2197)

Themes: Grace; ministry in daily life; morning, midday, evening, and night praise and prayer; characteristics of Jesus

The four verses of this new hymn parallel key qualities of Jesus with particular times of an ordinary day. The hope and joy that Jesus conveyed reflects the promise of a new day. Jesus, skilled in manual labor, working with eagerness and faith, offers inspiration while we are working. The grace and kindness Christ offered as friend warms our homecoming after a day's labor. The peace and serenity Jesus portrayed allows us to rest in peace.

This hymn is particularly appropriate to use in daily prayer and praise services (morning, midday, evening, night—see *The United Methodist Book of Worship*, 568-580). It also works well as a hymn to celebrate God's presence in our daily lives, not just in our worship. Invite those who would to reflect on these verses and pray them at the corresponding times of day.

Lord, prepare me to be a sanctuary (2164)

Themes: God's grace; our response to God

In eight simple measures, a very honest prayer is beautifully poured out in song. This sung prayer would be appropriate as a song of preparation before the spoken word (sermon or testimony) or as a response to the Word. It might be played instrumentally as a time of reflection after the spoken word. The tempo is slow ($\downarrow$ = 60) and the style is meditative. It is especially effective when sung *a cappella* in unison or parts. The Singer's and Accompaniment

Editions also include a modulation from D to E♭, as well as an extended choral ending. Use a small ensemble on the choral ending for a slower, softer, reflective conclusion.

Another appropriate use of this song would be during a time of prayer. Sing it one time and then continue to play it very softly during a spoken prayer. Conclude the prayer by singing it again with the modulation and choral ending.

Lord, we come to ask your blessing (2230)
Themes: Blessing; love; unity; the church

Here is a hymn about the love that Christians are to have for one another, with its source in God. It may be applied to the church or to a Christian marriage. It moves beyond the simple blessings of love, to sharing our gifts and forbearing one another. It may be used as a prayer for unity within a small study group, a congregation, a denomination, or ecumenically. Use it with the Epistle scriptures about unity among Christians. It would also be appropriate before a wedding or during the lighting of the unity candle.

To introduce this hymn, use a soloist, violin, or oboe. The congregation will be able to learn it relatively quickly as the first and third lines of melody are identical and the second and fourth differ only slightly. Guitar and bass may enhance the keyboard accompaniment.

Lord, you are more precious than silver (2065)
Themes: Grace of Jesus Christ; loving Christ above all (John 21:15)

An intimate chorus of worship of Christ, this song could be used in combination with such hymns as "My Jesus, I Love Thee" (UMH, 172). This would also be a good song to sing during a communion service, either as the elements are prepared or as the people commune. It would also be appropriate before, during, or after the offering.

To teach or lead the song, a choir or ensemble could sing it once in unison, adding harmonies on the repeat as the congregation joins. The instrumentation should be simple, perhaps just keyboard(s) and/or guitar(s), so as not to take away from the simple devotional message of the lyrics. A tempo of about 100 beats per minute would work nicely.

Love the Lord your God (2168)
Themes: Love for God; holiness

In this song the congregation is challenged to respond to God's love by loving God. Essentially, it states musically what Jesus refers to as the Great Commandment. It might work well to sing this before or as a response to the reading of the Gospel, especially one of the passages in which Jesus gives the Great Commandment (Matt. 22:37; Mark 12:30; Luke 10:27). This song would also be a call to prayer, leading into prayers of worship and love for God.

This chorus is especially appropriate for use with children, and they would lead the congregation beautifully in it. In addition, it lends itself to visual interpretation using sign language.

In a medley, this song could lead into "O How I Love Jesus" (UMH, 170). In this case it would help to lower the key to E♭ to facilitate a smooth key change to A♭ for "O How I Love Jesus."

Loving Spirit (2123)
Themes: Holy Spirit; presence of the Spirit; images of God

This hymn tells of the presence of the Spirit with us through all of life, loving and nurturing us like a parent. There are reminders of our baptism in the text (sign and promise) and of communion ("feed me with your very body"). So this hymn could be sung as preparation for baptism or communion, as well as a reminder of whose we are. Remember to end with the opening stanza, as the images come full circle.

The opening stanza might also be sung by itself as a call to prayer or preparation for confirmation or reaffirmation of baptism. The tune will be familiar to many as the communion hymn, "For the bread which you have broken." Keep it moving, in a gentle three beats per measure. Choirs may sing parts when singing it as service music or with the congregation.

Make me a channel of your peace (2171)
Themes: Peace; prayer; faith; service; giving; forgiveness

The *Prayer of St. Francis* flows from the heart in this flowing devotional setting. With peace as a recurring theme, in this song the congregation prays for social holiness. The song would function well as a framework around which to structure the Prayers of the People, with spoken prayers between the stanzas. It would also work in conjunction with "Lord, I Want to Be a Christian" (UMH, 402) or after "Spirit of the Living God" (UMH, 393) in a prayer medley. The latter combination follows personal holiness with social holiness.

The accompaniment is written for piano, but finger-picked guitar would also be effective. The tempo should be moderate (about $\downarrow$ = 62).

Make me a servant (2176)
Themes: Social holiness; servanthood; commitment and consecration; prayer and intercession

Based on the theme of servanthood found in Mark 10:43-45, Philippians 2:5-7, and John 13:14-16, this simple chorus would be appropriate anytime the lectionary calls for these readings. This song, accompanied by organ and or guitar, is also appropriate during a time of intercessory prayers. Sing it through once; then, as the instrumentalists repeat the song, have a time of spontaneous prayers for the needs of the community and the world, and for particular social issues. After several prayers have been offered, sing the chorus again. Repeat the process, ending with the chorus.

Use this chorus as a response during a Maundy Thursday service, especially if foot washing is emphasized.

Make us one, Lord (2224)
Themes: Unity; love; witness; Holy Spirit; community of faith

In this song the congregation prays for unity not just for its own sake, but as a witness to the world. It would work well to sing this song at the beginning or ending of a time of prayer. It would also flow well out of "In Christ There Is No East or West" (UMH, 548).

The jazz harmonies in the accompaniment add interest, while also providing a challenge. Because of this, a choir, worship team, or ensemble could sing it through twice before the congregation joins. The first time through, they could sing in unison, adding harmonies the second time and bringing in the congregation the third time through. The tempo should be unhurried, about 68 beats per minute.

May the God of hope go with us (2186)
Canto de Esperanza
Themes: God's care; faithfulness; commitment; ministry in daily life

This lively song from Argentina is a prayer for peace and justice, for all peoples and races. It reminds us of our calling to ministry, to pray and work with one another. It is a song of hope.

This song is appropriate for sending forth, for Peace with Justice Sunday, and for Human Relations Day. Instruments might include guitar and claves. Play the claves on the first beat of each measure. For additional variation, have one side of the congregation sing the first half of the stanza (eight measures), then have the other side sing the remainder of the stanza. The two sides may face each other as they sing. Everyone sings the refrain. Suggested tempo: ($\downarrow$ = 108).

May you run and not be weary (2281)
Theme: Sending forth

This song has been a favorite in many congregations for years. It is upbeat and simple, and a great way to send people into the world. Use it as a closing hymn or a sung congregational response to the benediction. Care should be taken not to sing it too fast. Take it a bit slower in order to give it a more gentle rock feel. Add many different instruments to this song as well, such as cello, flute, and saxophone. However, the beauty of the song is that it can be just as effective with only piano or guitar accompaniment.

Miren Qué Bueno (2231)
See "O look and wonder."

More like you (2167)
Themes: Commitment; service; discipleship
   This song is a prayer song, asking Jesus to give us his qualities of grace and mercy. It works well toward the end of the service, as a song of commitment and response to the Word. Use this song as a prayer response, either with prayers of intercession or as a call to prayer or prayer of confession. Visually, you may enhance this song with slides of current events that convey situations of anger, injustice, and conflict, or other situations in which we pray to be more like Jesus. Return to the congregation singing the refrain of the song. Follow it with another closing song, one that is very short and more upbeat, or use the optional extended ending in the Accompaniment Edition.

More Precious than Silver (2065)
See "Lord, you are more precious than silver."

Mothering God, you gave me birth (2050)
Themes: God's loving nature; comfort; communion; the Trinity
   We come to know God in many different ways, as our Creator, as our Savior, and as our Comfort. This hymn sings of God who gives us birth, who feeds us in communion, and who helps us grow, with images from the prayer life of a fifteenth-century woman of the church. Introduce it with care on Trinity Sunday or on Mother's Day, or as a prayer (with different voices reading the first two stanzas and all joining on the final stanza). The middle stanza might be pulled out as a communion chorus, repeated during the distribution.
   In addition to the lovely instrumental descant, accompaniment might include a string quartet as an option to keyboard. Let the quarter notes of the descant move the tempo in an unhurried, lyric manner.

My gratitude now accept, O God (2044)
Gracias, Señor
Themes: God's faithfulness; God's providential care; thanksgiving; praise
   This song of thanksgiving acknowledges that everything belongs to God and that from God's merciful hand flow all blessings for God's people. It is appropriate as an offertory hymn, which may be sung in its entirety as a thanksgiving prayer before the offertory, or the second stanza only may be sung after the offertory, using the last ending. The third stanza may be used as a call to worship, using the last ending.

This hymn is particularly appropriate for One Hour of Sharing (March). It is also appropriate for Stewardship Sunday (November) or for services that focus on the stewardship of gifts. It may also be used during Thanksgiving Day celebrations. Suggested tempo: ($\downarrow$ = 46).

My Jesus, My Savior (2074)
Themes: Praise; adoration

This popular praise song can be effectively used in almost any style of worship. It is very dramatic, and care needs to be used when singing it. The tendency is to sing too strongly from the beginning. Instead, sing it quietly and tenderly until the refrain. Sing the entire song twice, building in intensity as it is sung. Repeat the refrain again after the second time, and then close the song twice at the very end with "nothing compares to the promise I have in you."

Use this song to take people into a time of study about God's promises. Keep the music going, or be silent, as the congregation considers God's promises through scripture and meditation, then return to the refrain of the song one more time. On the repeat after the time of meditation, sing it quietly and tenderly rather than with the power of the earlier singing.

My life flows on (2212)
(How Can I Keep from Singing)
Themes: Hope in Christ; joy amid despair and strife

Even in times of tumult and strife, sadness and despair, storms and conflict, Christians have a song of joy and love to sing because Jesus lives and saves us. This text and tune will join others by this composer already well known to United Methodists: "Up from the Grave He Arose" (UMH, 322); "Nothing but the Blood" (UMH, 362); "I Need Thee Every Hour" (UMH, 397); "Shall We Gather at the River" (UMH, 723); and "Marching to Zion" (UMH, 733).

As with others in this gospel song genre, it should be sung spiritedly with a strong sense of the beat. The shaking of a handbell choir on the refrain might musically elaborate that text. A song leader may facilitate a congregation's learning the metrical changes by prompting phrase divisions and breathing points.

Stanza 3 provides an opportunity for contrast of text, style, and mood. As it speaks of the absence of joy and comfort and the gathering of darkness and night—a rather somber turn in this otherwise joyous hymn—the accompanist can lead the congregation more fully into this contrast by changing the key to G minor, playing all B's and E's as flatted notes while retaining the F#'s. The volume should be reduced and the tempo slowed, with a sense of *rubato*. The last stanza should abruptly return to the more joyful key of G major.

My life is in you, Lord (2032)
Themes: Adoration and praise of God; faith; hope; testimony; assurance and trust

Based on Deuteronomy 6:5, Philippians 1:21, and Colossians 1:27, this song confirms that God is our strength and hope. The worshiper is able to testify to this truth through the strong, high-energy style of this song ($\quarternote$ = 132-144).

The opening of the service, a response to the spoken word, or the sending forth are all appropriate places for this song. This is another example of a contemporary song that works well in combination with traditional hymns that celebrate the glory of the Triune God. Use in a medley with "Lord, I Lift Your Name on High" (2088) and "To God Be the Glory" (UMH, 98) (key of G major with a Latin beat).

My song is love unknown (2083)
Themes: The love of Christ; reconciliation with God in Christ

The "love unknown" here is the mystery of the Incarnation: how can God take on human flesh, and suffer and die for us? How can God love us that much? We cannot understand it, but we pour out our hearts in sung praise for it.

The succession of stanzas suggests a quiet beginning and thoughtful progression as the events of Holy Week are recounted. Individual stanzas of this hymn might be sung by soloist, choir, or congregation at the appropriate point as the biblical passages recalling Holy Week's events are read. The hymn is especially appropriate for Good Friday services.

The beautiful RHOSYMEDRE tune is unfamiliar to many congregations. Organists might introduce it by playing a simple one-note melody all the way through, repeating it with a doubled octave to accompany stanza 1, adding harmony only at stanza 2.

Nada Te Turbe (2054)
See "Nothing can trouble."

Noho Pū (2198)
See "Stay with me."

Nothing can trouble (2054)
Nada Te Turbe
Themes: Assurance; presence of God; hope; faith; providence of God

This hopeful prayer drawn from the words of St. Teresa de Jesús is a favorite of the Taizé Community, an ecumenical monastic order in southeastern France. Its simple, slightly syncopated rhythm should not be taken too slowly or allowed to drag. Think of the rhythm as the steady heartbeat of God reassuring the singer that indeed, *Solo Dios basta* ("God is sufficient"). It is best sung unaccompanied or with the minimal support of a guitar, cello, and flute. Additional responses for the song leader to be sung over the top of the congregation's part can be found in *Cantos de Taizé* (GIA Publications, Inc.). This adds effective variety to the repetitions. Consider singing this in Spanish. Many people are acquainted with this language and you may have members in your congregation for whom Spanish is their first language.

The most obvious use of this song is as a preparation for prayers of intercession. Singing it several times (at least three or four) prepares those gathered to offer their prayers before God. You might sing the last two measures (the second ending) as a brief congregational response to each intercession offered aloud. Another possibility is to sing this quietly during communion.

Now it is evening (2187)
Themes: Evening prayers; service; comfort

Comfortable images of evening are found in the first half of these stanzas, but the second half calls us from our comfort into acts of service. Approach this hymn simply in both accompaniment (piano, guitar) and vocal style. A soloist might introduce the first three stanzas with all joining on the last. Invite the congregation to share signs of peace and greeting following the last verse. Use a moderate waltz tempo ($\downarrow$ = 108).

If you have evening services, consider using this song during Advent with the lighting of the Advent wreath candles. The last word of each stanza can be attached to the four candles.

This text may also be sung to the tune BUNESSAN, which we use with the hymn "Morning Has Broken" (UMH, 145). Combining this evening hymn with a tune that we associate with the morning can express God's presence with us through the entire day.

Now praise the hidden God of love (2027)
Themes: God's love at all stages of human life; the Christian community

This short hymn is a reflection of our identity as a Christian community, made up of people of all ages who find their common calling in God's love. It is especially appropriate on those occasions that observe the major stages of Christian development: birth, baptism, confirmation, Sunday school promotion, commissioning and dedication of leaders.

The simplicity and beauty of this folk song suggest some use with instruments, especially a flute, oboe, or recorder. The melody could be effectively played by an unaccompanied instrument as introduction, or sung by an unaccompanied singer or unison choir.

Effective presentation of this hymn might include having a young adult read stanza 1, a child or a youth read stanza 2, and an older adult read stanza 3, each preceded by an instrumental rendering of the melody. The congregation may then follow by singing all three stanzas.

This tune may already be familiar to many in congregations as "Gift of Love" (UMH, 408). The notation of the tune in this setting suggests a slightly faster tempo ($\stackrel{\downarrow}{}$ = 64) than in the other hymn. In addition, there are subtle changes in the melody from the other hymn; however, these changes are ones the congregation will be inclined to sing naturally, so there is no need to call attention to the differences.

O blessed spring (2076)
Themes: The Christian life; praise for the mystery of life; funerals and memorial services

This hymn is a progressive commentary on the life of every human being, comparing the stages of life to the four seasons of the year: spring, summer, autumn and winter. One obvious use of the hymn would be in a funeral service, where the singing of the hymn would both reflect on the mystery of death and also the hope of every Christian: eternal life in Jesus Christ.

The tune, GIFT OF LOVE, is an arrangement by Hal H. Hopson of a traditional English melody that is well known by many congregations and particularly suited to this beautiful text. The descant can be sung either by a soloist or by the choir. An obbligato instrument, such as flute or oboe, could also perform the descant. Guitar accompaniment would work particularly well with this setting and guitar chords are printed along with the music.

O freedom (African American spiritual) (2194)
Themes: Liberation; strength in tribulation; trust; hope and healing

Under the power of the Holy Spirit, we are granted true freedom. Unfortunately, humans continue to enslave and oppress one another, and there are always reasons to call in prayer upon the Almighty for freedom from moaning and weeping, as long as people anywhere in the world seek to be freed from any form of tyranny. In addition, there are other psychological and physical enslavements that people of faith experience, such as drugs, mental illnesses, or incurable diseases. Thus, the prayers of the people should include "O Freedom" for all people of the world. Use this song as a prayer of intercession or for healing. It is also an appropriate selection for Peace with Justice Sunday and Human Relations Day.

It will be difficult to use this spiritual in the liturgical context without affirming the importance of its origin and continuous use in the Civil Rights Movement and in any situation where there is oppression, human against human, in any form. The liberation-freedom motif provides an opportunity for intercessory prayers for healing.

O freedom (South Africa) (2192)

Themes: Freedom; hope; Advent; assurance

This lively South African freedom song combines the hope for political freedom from oppression to the coming of Jesus. In many ways it is ideal for Advent. Singing this song each Sunday throughout the season of Advent—first by the choir and then by the people—can add a sense of vitality to this important time in the Christian Year. "Freedom Is Coming" can be used as a choir processional during almost any season of the Christian Year or as a response to appropriate sermons.

Teach the congregation the lower three parts or simply the alto line. Have the choir fill in the remaining parts. At first, use a soloist on the soprano part after the other parts are secure. Establish the basic rhythm and harmony with the lower three parts by singing them through once. Upon the repetition, add the melody. Sing unaccompanied if possible, a common practice among many South African tribes. The only accompaniment would be clapping on the beat while swaying to the rhythm. If the choir is prepared to lead, the congregation will learn easily. It is not necessary to have books in hand if the congregation learns to listen to the leader and melody for the word cues indicating a change in the text. Establish a firm, lively beat and maintain it to the end. On the second stanza, the song leader can also add appropriate Advent phrases such as "prepare the way" or "make straight the paths" or "the valleys will rise" from Isaiah 40:3-4.

O God beyond all praising (2009)

Themes: Praise of God in all things; awe and wonder; our need to praise; commitment

This melody from *The Planets* by Gustav Holst is majestic and delightful to sing. Before the service or during the offertory, the text could be used as meditation while listening to a small orchestra or recording of the music. A trumpet or French horn might reinforce the singing. The melody shifts between higher and lower ranges, and would lend itself to being sung as follows: high voices on the first two lines of the text; lower voices on the next three lines of the text; ending with high voices on the final line.

The second stanza of the text suggests that, in addition to a general hymn of praise, this hymn might be used as a prayer hymn of commitment, during communion services, or during a Wesley covenant service (or at New Year's).

O Holy Spirit, Root of life (2121)

Themes: Holy Spirit; Pentecost

This hymn brings together the writings of a twelfth-century mystic and the music of a fifteenth-century melody, both of which remain important to us in the twenty-first century. The images of the text help us to understand the various aspects and workings of the Holy Spirit. In three short stanzas, there are no fewer than a dozen different images of the Spirit—a wealth of inspiration for liturgical dancers!

Accompanists may be tempted to play this hymn too fast, with a feeling of one strong beat per measure, resulting in the richness of the text being lost for lack of time to understand it as it is being sung. Allow each measure to have its full three beats. The third stanza's text can lead to a powerfully soaring accompaniment, perhaps an alternate harmonization.

O how he loves you and me (2108)

Themes: Grace; love; sacrifice; the cross; hope

This song draws our attention to the gift of love given to us by Jesus Christ. It also serves to unify the congregation as those whom Christ loves. The first stanza might be used at a time of greeting or fellowship. As people greet one another, the choir could sing the song; as the congregation returns to their seats, they could join in the singing. Both stanzas are particularly effective in a communion service, pointing to Christ's sacrifice as the source of our hope. To lessen any ambiguity, the word *he* could be replaced by *Christ* in the first two lines of the first stanza.

On this hymnlike song, the organ may be effective, as would piano and/or guitar. A quiet finger-picked guitar with a keyboard reinforcing the voice parts would also sound very nice on this song.

O look and wonder (2231)

Miren Qué Bueno

Themes: The community of faith; unity

This lively song from Argentina has its scriptural base in Psalm 133. It reminds us what a blessing it is for the community of the faithful to worship together. It can be used as gathering music while the congregation arrives, as a praise song, or as a call to worship. It may also be used for the passing of the peace: After the congregation sings the refrain once, a leader or the choir can continue singing the stanzas while the people greet one another, singing along in the refrain.

This song is appropriate for Human Relations Day services or celebrations (January).

It would be good for the congregation to sing the short refrain in Spanish. Since the line repeats, the leader could sing it first, then the congregation follows.

A guitar may be used for accompaniment, and claves are also appropriate:

Suggested tempo: (♩ = 92).

O Lord, hear my prayer (2200)
Themes: Prayer; petition

This selection is from the Taizé Community, an ecumenical monastic order in southeastern France. Extended silence is a part of the three daily prayer services in the community. This selection is ideal for either preparing for or responding to a period of silence in worship. It can also be used to prepare the prayers of the people.

Sing unaccompanied, if possible. A cello, guitar, flute, or oboe also add variety and support without becoming obtrusive. Instrumental parts are available in the Accompaniment Edition. Plan to sing this selection at least four times or until the congregation has centered on the prayer. Try to vary the accompaniment slightly each time the cycle is repeated.

O Lord, our Lord, how majestic is your name (2023)
Themes: The majesty of Christ; names for Jesus; praise; adoration

This song is a great praise medley opener, with much energy and an engaging, recognizable tune. Creativity may come with use of various instrumentation. Involve some rhythm instruments: Use a tambourine to accent the downbeat at the beginning of every four measures during the first half of the song (through "in all the earth") and then at the downbeat of every two measures from that point to the end. You can also add conga drums or even timpani, for a more majestic sound! But take care—this song has a tendency to become a speeding train. Try to keep a steady pace (about ♩ = 80). At the end of the song, repeat the final names for Jesus, "Prince of peace, mighty God," as a stronger conclusion for the song.

O Lord, your tenderness (2143)
Themes: God's mercy; healing; praise; pardon and assurance

The music of this prayer song reflects well the character of tenderness attributed to God. The melody—tender and gentle—should be sung just that way. Introduce the chorus by playing the melody on a flute, unaccompanied. The second time through, add a soft organ and let the worship leader sing it as a solo. The third time, invite the congregation to sing. This song would be a wonderful choral response to the sermon. It would also be an appropriate song for the congregation to sing during communion.

O Lord, you're beautiful (2064)
Themes: Assurance; trust; care and God's grace

The beauty of the Psalms is evident in the melody of this contemporary prayer chorus. It can be used as a preparation for prayer, sung between spoken prayers, or as a sung prayer response. Make use of its slow reverent style by playing it with soft instrumentation while congregational prayers are being offered (♩ = 64).

The second stanza, not often published, would work well for a service of healing. Appropriate songs for a medley are: "O Lord, Your Tenderness" (2143); "All I Need Is You" (2080); and "Open Our Eyes" (2086).

O-So-So (2232)

See "Come now, O Prince of Peace."

Oh, I know the Lord's laid his hands on me (2139)

Themes: Affirmation; assurance; healing; witness and testimony

The refrain of this spiritual is a jubilant confirmation of the divine presence, power, and personal "anointing touch" of Christ the Lord. If it is new to a congregation, the choir or a soloist/song leader can introduce the refrain with fervor and invite the congregation to join in the singing three or four times until the refrain is familiar. Verses are added by the soloist in a call and response format as directed by the soloist or choir director. The structure is such that this song can be taught with or without an accompanying instrument. Accompaniment, which incorporates rhythmic clapping, should be introduced after the chorus has been learned. People may clap on each beat of every measure, or on alternate beats; beginning with either the first or second beat of each measure.

Oh, I woke up this morning (2082)

Themes: Affirmation; trust and dedication

The term *stayed* as used in this text means firmly lodged, deeply rooted, and confirmed. Thus, one whose mind is "stayed on Jesus" is firmly lodged, unwavering, steadfast, deeply rooted, and committed to the teachings of Jesus the Christ. The biblical reference is the promise of Isaiah 26:3*a*: "Those of steadfast mind you keep in peace—in peace because they trust in you" (NRSV), which is translated "whose mind is stayed on thee" (KJV). To wake up with one's mind "stayed on Jesus" means that the day's journey will be under divine control. It will be impossible to hate anyone, or fear the wiles of the devil because "Jesus is the captain of your mind," as expressed in the text. Use this hymn as an opening hymn of praise or as a hymn for morning prayer.

The call and response structure throughout this spiritual will facilitate the teaching-learning process, and will also encourage congregational participation.

On bended knee (2207)

Theme: Prayer

This is a meditative song of prayer and confession, easily used during a focused time of prayer in the worship service. It works especially well to be sung at a time when people may wish to get up and physically move to another place for prayer, such as to the altar or to a prayer station for special prayer or for anointing and healing. Another option would be to use this song during communion.

This song is very heartfelt and brings a person into a deep connection with the human desire of seeking to be in touch God's healing power. Singing it can help a person name the fact that there are wounds buried deep inside, waiting to be released. Sing it very simply, with not much instrumentation, perhaps only piano or guitar. You can repeat this song several times, and move into other songs of prayer and confession as well.

One God and Father of Us All (2240)
See "All the gifts that God has given."

One heart, one Spirit (2227)
Themes: Unity; the church as the Body of Christ
This song focuses on the community's relationship with Christ. It calls the church to be unified under the Lordship of Jesus and to honor and glorify Jesus in our lives as a church. "We Are the Body of Christ" is a very singable tune. The chorus works well as an ending song for an opening praise medley. Another use could be the end of the service, as a sending forth. This song would also tie in well thematically with "They'll Know We Are Christians by Our Love" (2223) and with "The Family Prayer Song" (2188).

One holy night in Bethlehem (2097)
Themes: Jesus' birth; Mary and Joseph; Christmas Eve
This hymn can make a charming addition to your Christmas Eve worship. Sing it during a "living nativity scene," or intersperse stanzas with the reading of the Christmas story from the Gospels.

Consider alternating between adults and/or youth singing the stanzas, and children and/or congregation singing the refrain. Another plan might be to have a female soloist, "Mary," sing the refrain after stanza 2, and a man or group of men whistle the refrain melody after stanza 3. Keep the tempo joyous (about ♩ = 112-116).

If you use the SATB final refrain, its tempo may need to be slower. Slow down the end of stanza 4 as you approach the refrain to signal the slower tempo to the congregation.

Open our eyes, Lord (2086)
Themes: Prayer and intercession; walking with God
This popular prayer chorus is most often used as a preparation for or response to prayer, but would also be very appropriate as a song of prepara-

tion before the reading of scriptures or the sermon. It is based on Isaiah 50:4-5 and Matthew 5:8. Begin the chorus by reading the Matthew scripture during the introduction.

Keep the song flowing at a moderate pace ($\quarternote$ = 100). Solo out the melody on a soft instrument or play the chorus while a unison prayer is read. Several songs that can be combined with it are "As the Deer" (2025); "Sanctuary" (2164); and "Holy Ground" (2272).

Our Father in heaven (2278)
Theme: The Lord's Prayer

Jim Strathdee's moving setting of the Lord's Prayer is strong and vibrant, the honest prayer of a pilgrim people. The congregation doesn't need music for this one, and the leader will be better off knowing it "by heart" if possible, so that the interaction of call and response can be most effective. Given a song leader to sing the "call" and a strong song leader to lead the people in the "response," the music almost sings itself. No one who has heard the Strathdees sing this with driving drum accompaniment will ever forget it. Note that the text returns to the opening lines at the conclusion of the prayer.

Our God is an awesome God (2040)
Themes: God's glory and power; call to worship

This song calls the congregation to worship by drawing attention to God's power and transcendence. There are several scripture references for this song, so it could also be used effectively as a congregational response to the reading of these or other scripture texts. Another variation would be for a group of children or youth to sing it, inviting the congregation to join after a time or two.

Try repeating the refrain several times, changing the accompaniment or leaving it out entirely on some repetitions. Begin in a slower tempo with a sense of awe and wonder and build in intensity and increase tempo as the refrain is repeated. Drop the keyboard accompaniment at the closing repetitions of the refrain, using only percussion. A song leader or small ensemble could sing the verses (included in the Singer's and Accompaniment Editions of this Supplement). Although simple and repetitive, this song has a majestic feel to it, and should be sung powerfully.

Out of the depths (2136)
Themes: Alienation from God, others, and our own bodies; healing and wholeness

In this text, Ruth Duck leads us from fears and painful memories to lament, and from lament to the presence of God's healing within loving community. The text will speak to and for congregations in services of healing, services of lament, and services of reconciliation. It will have special meaning in times of prayer for those who are seriously ill (the first alternative wording noted was written for AIDS healing services) or for those who have been abused. The text as it stands, however, relates to any Christian group seeking to embody genuine community.

The haunting melody should be introduced using the melody line only (whether by a solo instrument, a keyboard, or by a solo voice). It should be sung softly and reflectively at an unhurried tempo. The open fifth in the first measure resonates with the opening measure of Martin Luther's "Out of the Depths I Cry to You" (UMH, 515). While both Luther and Duck have written texts of lament (of which there are precious few), they have very different themes, although both have their scriptural basis in Psalm 130:1.

Over my head (2148)

Themes: Affirmation and assurance of the existence and continual presence of God; trust and faith

"There must be a God somewhere!" There is comfort in knowing that God is somewhere, out of the way of earthly confinement and human interference. God's continual presence is the focus of this spiritual composed by a community whose earthly existence needed this kind of assurance. This is true for each age, thus allowing this spiritual to remain contemporary, relevant, and easily accessible to congregations. In addition to the countermelody added by John Bell, congregations might add earlier texts: "Over my head, I hear singing," "I see glory," "I feel love." This song can be taught and performed effectively *a cappella*. It can be used during the time of gathering, as a choral call to worship, or during a time of praise.

People need the Lord (2244)

Themes: Mission; witness; redemption; grace

This song calls God's people to share Christ with all who don't know him. It could be used before "Here I Am, Lord" (UMH, 593), as a response to a sermon calling the congregation to mission in their community and the world, or as a theme for a service centered on evangelism, witness, and missions. This song could also serve as musical framework for a time of prayer, especially prayers for healing or commissioning evangelists or missionaries. To make it more personal for the congregation, try substituting "We all" for "People" each time the word "People" occurs in the song.

The accompaniment may consist of piano only, or guitars and percussion could join in. Depending on the mood of the service, an organ might help to increase the dynamic contrast in the song, adding to the feeling of passion for those who need the Lord. A slight *ritard* in the second measure of the first ending would be effective. The tempo should be approximately 84 to 88 beats per minute.

Perdón, Señor **(2134)**
See "Forgive us, Lord."

Please enter my heart, hosanna (2154)
Themes: Spiritual rebirth; the new creature; salvation; invitation

This chorus is a beautiful response to Christ's invitation to become "new creatures." It would be most appropriate to sing following the sermon. The syncopated rhythms should not be overemphasized, but should flow naturally and unobtrusively. It is a prayer and should be sung as a prayer. The lyrics are simple and repetitive enough that after the congregation has sung it several times, they should be able to close their eyes and make it a heartfelt prayer. Include a note explaining that the word *Hosanna* literally means "save us now."

This song would also be a fitting choice to use during a time of prayer at the altar. The refrain and the coda ending may also be used as a response to the lighting of the Advent candles.

Praise our God above (2061)
Themes: Praise; thanksgiving; Creation; harvest; gratitude

Thanksgiving is a universal expression. This Confucian chant has been Christianized by pairing it with a text of praise to the one God. The melody has its own natural beauty and should not be harmonized, especially not in a Western manner. Support the melody with a single reed or flute stop on the organ or with an oboe or flute. It is also appropriate to embellish the melody slightly in an heterophonic manner. (*Heterophony* is the playing of a melody in an embellished or ornamented form while it is simultaneously being played or sung in its original or more simple version.) If a harmonic foundation is required, consider supporting the melody with an open fifth on C and G.

This lovely hymn of praise may be introduced by the children to the congregation. Play the melody first on a flute, recorder, or oboe. Have the children sing the first stanza and then invite the congregation to join them on the second stanza. It is appropriate anytime a hymn of praise is needed, but especially during the harvest or in anticipation of the Thanksgiving season. This song reminds us that God's abundance extends throughout the earth to all nations. Thanksgiving for the abundance of the harvest is a natural expression of humanity.

Praise, praise, praise the Lord (2035)
Themes: Praise; thanksgiving; gratitude

Sing this energetic praise song from Cameroon in West Africa at a stately tempo (no more than $\quartnote = 64\text{-}72$). Start with a solo voice on the first phrase and then invite all the people to sing on the repeat. Do the same with the second half of the song. Unlike Western musical practice, emphasize the final "ia" of the word "alleluia" with a strong accent. The congregation might enjoy swaying to the beat in the following manner: small step right, close with left foot; small step left, close with right foot. This step would take a complete measure. As you close with both the left or right foot, add a clap. Layer on percussion instruments, such as tambourine, maracas, claves, and bongos one at a time, each with their own pattern, until you create a polyrhythmic (multilayered rhythmic effect) accompaniment for the singing. The song is quite effective when sung unaccompanied.

"Praise, Praise, Praise the Lord" is an effective choir processional. It is also an excellent song to frame prayers of praise and thanksgiving. Following each expression of gratitude, sing the last line only as a congregational response. The song is an excellent response for psalms of praise, such as Psalms 100 and 150.

Praise the Lord with the sound of trumpet (2020)
Themes: Praise; music recognition; Creation

This joyous song is very accessible to adults and children alike. It is close-ly related to Psalm 150 but it can also be used anytime a general praise song is needed. It makes an excellent call to worship or opening worship song.

In informal settings, you might ask the singers to sing only the phrase "praise the Lord," adding three hand claps with these three words. When singing as a round, it may be best to repeat stanza 1 as a round after singing stanza 2, so as not to obscure the text of stanza 2. The congregation might sing part 1, with the choir or song leader singing part 2.

Use various instruments to accompany. An instrument (flute or trumpet) could also be the second part in the round. Less experienced instrumentalists may be able to play the melody of measures 1-7. These measures appear three times in each stanza, giving them plenty to play but less to learn.

Praise the name of Jesus (2066)
Themes: Praise; call to worship; witness; God's character

This medium tempo song works well as a call to worship. It also will work well as a follow-up to "Blessed Assurance" (UMH, 369), especially in a service that allows people to share their faith stories with the congregation. It also may be used as a call to prayer. When used early in the service it might be sung with strength. If used as a call to prayer it should be sung quietly and prayerfully. The congregation could sing "We praise your name, Lord Jesus. . . . You're our Rock" to corporately focus on Christ. Another use for the song would be as a children's song. For instance, they could sing it before or after a children's message.

The text points to the connection between the God of the Old Testament ("Rock," "Fortress," "Deliverer") and Jesus.

Praise the source of faith and learning (2004)

Themes: Praise; faith; learning; growth in faith; wonder of God; God as source of all knowledge

This hymn is appropriate for confirmation, Christian Education Sunday (including adults), Student Sunday, for sending college students off, and with the biblical story of Jesus growing in faith (Luke 2:39-40). However, deeper than a simple hymn about growing, this text confesses our arrogance about knowledge, reminding us that learning always needs to be tempered and strengthened by faith. In contrast, the confession in the third stanza cautions us against an unthinking faith. It may be followed by the interlude as a brief time of confession for the times when we have used faith without knowledge and harmed others. Thus, the text can be powerfully used whenever deeper issues of science and faith or varieties of religions are engaged.

The river images in the final stanza suggest a flowing tempo throughout. In addition to singing, consider using the text as a prayer and meditation text.

Praise to the Lord (2029)

Themes: Praise; glory of God; God's reversal of the human condition; God's love for the weak and lowly

This warm hymn works as a praise chorus or like the songs of Taizé for meditation and repetition, as a call to worship, an introit, with Psalm 113, the Magnificat (Luke 1:46b-55) and the Song of Hannah (1 Sam. 2:1-10), or during the distribution of communion. Teach the refrain first, with choir or soloists on the verses so that people can hear how the words fit differently on each stanza. Sing in parts if possible (invite singers to harmonize as they grow comfortable) or with wind instruments on the parts, with one beat per measure.

This hymn moves from praise of God to reminders of how God calls us to live. It is appropriate in services focused on the poor and less privileged in the community, and how Christians reach out to love as we have been loved.

Praise ye the Lord (2010)

Themes: Praise; adoration; all Creation in praise

This setting of Psalm 150 in an African American gospel style evokes imaginative, unfettered, and unencumbered praise with its driving vocal rhythm, repeated refrain, and aggressive keyboard accompaniment. This psalm is appropriate as an opening hymn of praise, as a response to the sermon, and when Psalm 150 is used in worship.

A song leader should introduce the refrain to the congregation in a call and response manner, with the assistance of the choir so that part singing can be encouraged. The verses should be sung initially by a song leader or by unison voices, and later by the congregation. Rhythmic clapping, with accented second and fourth beats, can be added with careful demonstration after the congregation gets the feel for the entire song.

Praise you (2003)

Themes: Praise; prayer; personal reflection; commitment; aspiration

This is a simple and beautiful setting of Psalm 119:175. Its slow, reflective mood would be appropriate during a time of prayer, a time of reflection following the spoken word, or a time of personal commitment. Suggested choral parts and leader stanzas are in the Singer's and Accompaniment Editions. Another option might be to begin with a solo voice and add other voices as the song progresses.

This song lends itself very well to dance interpretation. Simple hand motions or sign language could be used with the congregation. If used as an opening song of praise, the dancers could process with items (e.g., candles, fabric) to be placed on the altar. Then the song could be repeated at the end of the service as the dancers remove items from the altar. Keep all movement slow and fluid to reflect the mood of the text.

Prayers of the People (2201)

See "Lord, let your kingdom come."

Righteous and holy (2018)

Themes: Praise and worship; adoration

"Honor and Praise" is a great chorus to use at the opening of worship and during communion. Its short, repetitious form makes it easy to learn. Introduce it by having the accompanist play the second phrase ("We come before you with honor and praise"). Have the worship leader sing that phrase and then invite the congregation to sing it together. Then proceed with the chorus, treating that second phrase as a response. The worship leader would sing lines 1, 3, and 5 through 7. The congregation would join in singing lines 2, 4 and 8. This approach would work well during communion.

Rise Up, Shepherd, and Follow (2096)

See "There's a star in the East."

Sacred the body (2228)

Themes: Body as temple of the Holy Spirit; diversity; love

Reflecting 1 Corinthians 3:16-17, Ruth Duck's text celebrates the holiness of each person's body as a temple of the Holy Spirit. Diversity and relationship are both honored. The third stanza speaks to the widespread problems of battering and abuse as violations of the sacred. The hymn may also be used in services that focus on the nature of the church as a community of love and respect.

The tune is very singable. A folklike quality may be enhanced by the use of guitar accompaniment. The 9/8 time signature makes a black gospel piano accompaniment effective also. Do not hurry the tempo; rather, feel the pulsing of each eighth note. Unite each ten syllables (avoiding the temptation to divide the phrases into two groups of five syllables each).

Sanctuary (2164)
See "Lord, prepare me to be a sanctuary."

Sanctus (2256)
See "Holy, holy, holy Lord."

Santo (2019)
See "Holy."

Santo, santo, santo (2007)
See "Holy, holy, holy."

Sent out in Jesus' name (2184)
Enviado Soy de Dios
Themes: Commitment; discipleship; ministry in daily life

This songs speaks of the privilege given to the faithful to create a world of love, justice, and peace. It reminds us of our responsibility to do the work that even the angels cannot do. It serves well as a hymn of commitment, as response to the Word, or as sending forth.

With its focus on the spreading of the good news and the building of the kingdom of justice and peace, this song is appropriate for Peace with Justice Sunday. It is also appropriate for the season after Pentecost.

Guitar accompaniment is suitable. The use of claves on the first and third beats also works well. Suggested tempo: ($\downarrow$ = 92).

She comes sailing on the wind (2122)
Themes: Holy Spirit; Creation; salvation history; the Annunciation of Mary; the baptism of Jesus; the presence of the Spirit

"She" refers to the Holy Spirit, present at Creation (stanza 1), through salvation history (stanza 2), with Mary as Jesus is announced (stanza 3), and at the river Jordan when Jesus is baptized. Stanza 5 might be interpreted as Resurrection or the wind and fire of Pentecost. Emphasize the hymn's biblical basis for those who question the pronouns.

Teach the congregation the refrain, and have soloists sing the stanzas. Note that the refrain comes at the beginning, after stanza 2, after stanza 4, and at the end, after stanza 5 (stanzas 1 and 2, then 3 and 4 are sung without the refrain between). Double the bass line with an instrument and play the accompaniment on keyboard, soloing out the melody to begin. Use as an invocation at the beginning of worship, as a prayer hymn, or with selected stanzas to relate to scripture.

Shepherd me, O God (2058)

Themes: God's providential care, strength, and comfort in times of trouble

A fresh and somewhat haunting setting of Psalm 23, this refrain is appropriate when the lectionary calls for the psalm. The verses are found in the Singer's and Accompaniment Editions, and may be sung by a song leader, small ensemble, or choir. The Singer's Edition also includes vocal parts for the refrain. Make sure there is a strong voice leading the congregation in the melody if these parts are used.

The text of Psalm 23 may also be read in sections with the refrain serving as the congregation's musical response. See *The United Methodist Hymnal* for possible placement of the refrain (#137 and p. 754). The reading and singing may be a smoother act of worship if the accompaniment is played softly under the spoken text.

Shine, Jesus, shine (2173)

Themes: Renewal and revival of the church; God's presence with us

This highly energetic song based on Ephesians 5:2, 8-10, 14 calls us to walk as children of light: "For once you were darkness, but now in the Lord you are light" (v. 8). Play the first two measures of the stanza ending two times at a quick tempo ($\downarrow$ = 120) for the introduction. Give it a bright, energetic sound. Then slow the tempo down ($\downarrow$ = 108) in the last two measures of the stanza ending as preparation for the more fluid stanzas. In the last two measures of each stanza, return to the original tempo for the refrain.

This song is perfect for a service developed around missions or a renewal/revival of the church. It could be combined with the hymn "We've a Story to Tell to the Nations" (UMH, 569—lower to the key of E major). It also works well as a closing song almost anytime of the year.

Shout to the Lord (2074)

See "My Jesus, My Savior."

Since Jesus Came into My Heart (2140)

See "What a wonderful change."

Sing a new song to the Lord (2045)

Themes: Praise; singing; joy; salvation; nature; Incarnation

This lively hymn of praise lends itself to several ways of teaching. Teach the final line as a refrain and have soloists sing the opening lines of each stanza. You also might speak the text in rhythm, congregation echoing leader, and then add melody. Alternately, sing it antiphonally (with one group leading and another group echoing), as the second line echoes the first and the third line contains an echo within itself. Teenagers and older children may find that this text and rhythm make a good speech choir piece. Small percussion instruments can add to the excitement and the feeling of two beats per measure.

Congregations attempting to be more inclusive in their references to God will want to decide if they are using this text within a focus on the Godhead or on Jesus, and then change the masculine pronouns to God or Christ, accordingly.

Sing alleluia to the Lord (2258)

Themes: Holy Communion; adoration and praise; worship

This hauntingly beautiful chorus, set in a minor tonality, would be appropriate anytime a reflective, quiet song is called for in the order of worship—especially an evening vespers, prayer service, or celebration of communion. When singing the additional lyrics the song leader may sing the first phrase as a solo to indicate which text is to be sung. Use the new text on the first two phrases, then "sing alleluia" on the middle phrases, returning to the new text for the last phrase. For example,

> In Christ the world has been redeemed (repeat)
> Sing alleluia, sing alleluia,
> In Christ the world has been redeemed.

As the congregation sings the melody, the descant could be used in a variety of ways. It could be performed by a soloist, the choir, a children's choir, a soft solo stop on the organ, or by a flute or other obbligato instrument. It could also be played by handbells. Place the bell ringers in the balcony, narthex, or some out of the way place to create a distant echo effect.

Siyahamba (2235-a, 2235-b)

See "We are marching in the light of God" (2235-b).

Sólo Tú Eres Santo (2077)

See "You alone are holy."

Some glad morning (2282)
Theme: Death and eternal life

This hymn expresses the spirituality of older persons who remember it fondly from their youth and persons whose lives have been hard and for whom the hope of heaven gives them strength to endure. It may also be used at funeral and memorial services. It is a happy song, not a mournful one, and there is nothing inappropriate about singing it with enjoyment. It is most effectively sung in harmony.

If you have a time of informal worship when you invite people to sing their favorites and even bring instruments from home to play along, this is a favorite of guitar, banjo and bass players, drummers, and fiddlers, because it gives them the natural subdivided backbeat that is such an important part of the rural, Southern, white, gospel tradition.

Someone asked the question (2144)
Themes: God's love and grace for all of God's Creation; witness and testimony

This popular gospel song by Kirk Franklin is a testimony of faith in Almighty God, who frees believers to sing with their voices and with their lives. The text of the refrain is reminiscent of the song, "His Eye Is on the Sparrow" (2146), but is more in keeping with contemporary modes of vocal expression. The theological awareness that is strongly emphasized is God's concern for all Creation—*even* for the sparrow—assuring us of God's concern for humankind. Knowing this keeps one singing, even beyond the grave (Matt. 10:26-31 and Luke 12:4-7).

In congregations where this song is unfamiliar, it should be introduced as an anthem by the choir and gradually worked into the congregation's repertoire by involving the congregation in the singing of the refrain.

Somos Uno en Cristo (2229)
See "We are one in Christ Jesus."

Song of Hope (2186)
Canto de Esperanza
See "May the God of hope go with us."

Spirit of God (2117)
Theme: The Holy Spirit

This beautiful hymn by Steve Garnaas-Holmes is set in a contemporary worship style and is a prayer to the Holy Spirit for indwelling, peace, and healing. With five individual stanzas, a refrain with a descant, and an optional four-part choral arrangement of stanza 3, this hymn is extremely versatile and will give the creative worship leader many opportunities and combinations. The refrain can stand on its own as a separate chorus and can be repeated as many times as is fitting, with or without the descant. When singing the hymn, try using the optional third stanza for choir alone, *a cappella*. In addition, the final Alleluia of the optional third stanza could be used by the choir as a prayer response.

Spirit, Spirit of gentleness (2120)
Themes: The Holy Spirit; Pentecost

"Spirit, Spirit of Gentleness" would be appropriate to sing anytime the theme of the Holy Spirit is used in a service. The third stanza would be especially appropriate on Pentecost Sunday. The text is beautiful and very descriptive. You might have someone interpret the text through dance or American Sign Language as a soloist sings the stanzas. The congregation could join on the refrain. Another option is to have a children's choir sing the refrain. Guitar accompaniment works well with this song.

Star-Child (2095)
Themes: Jesus' coming; Advent; Christmas; justice

Shirley Erena Murray has combined symbolic and metaphorical verses with an extremely simple and straightforward refrain text. This is a Christmas text that can comfortably be used by all during Advent.

Introduce the hymn by having soloists sings stanzas 1-4 with the congregation joining on stanza 5. The congregation might also join in singing the refrain after it has been sung several times. The tempo should be about ♩ = 96. Vary the accompaniment on each stanza: organ, then guitar, then piano. Handbells could also play the accompaniment. A simple handbell or other instrumental part can be fashioned from the "alto" part of the accompaniment. Let the final stanza have a grand and expansive tempo and accompaniment.

There is a fine choral arrangement of this hymn by the hymn's composer, Carlton R. Young. It is available from Hope Publishing Company.

Stay with me (2198)
Noho Pū
Themes: Assurance; patience; spiritual vigilance; Holy Week

The text of this brief selection is drawn from the Passion narrative as found in Matthew 26. It is a chant from the Taizé Community in France that is designed to center the congregation in prayer, especially on Maundy Thursday or Good Friday. The close harmonies are logical and easily learned by a choir. They add a harmonic tension that symbolizes the agony of Christ's Passion and the anxiety felt by the disciples while they were with Jesus in the Garden of Gethsemane. Sing unaccompanied if possible or with the support of a light cello, violin, or flute. Sing at least five times, allowing the worshiper to center on Christ's agony as he pleaded with his Father to "let this cup pass from" him.

While it can be sung during any service where a prayer for vigilance is needed, it is most appropriate during a Maundy Thursday or Good Friday service. It would complement a service based on the Stations at the Cross as found in *The United Methodist Book of Worship.*

Stay with us (2199)
Themes: The presence, comfort, and healing of Christ

In such simple words and such short phrases, this hymn sings our prayers in times of loneliness, suffering, pain, loss, and death. A quiet flute or oboe playing the solo melody with soft accompaniment would prepare the hearts and quiet the spirits of the worshipers before they sing the hymn. An effective two-part *a cappella* version could be improvised by having the men's voices sing the first half of a stanza on the note G, moving to a dominant D at measure 4 (4/4 meter), singing that D for the remainder of the stanza, and returning to the tonic G on the last note.

The shifting of the meter from 4/4 to 2/4 to 4/4 to 3/4, and back to 4/4 should not be a deterrent to learning this hymn. These rhythms are quite natural to the text, and allow for natural breathing at the phrase points.

Sunday's palms are Wednesday's ashes (2138)
Themes: Lent; repentance; Ash Wednesday; confession

This hymn refers to the custom of burning the palm branches from the previous Palm Sunday (around eleven months ago) for Ash Wednesday. Thus, it is very appropriate for that service, as a prayer of confession. But consider also using it throughout Lent perhaps as a weekly prayer of confession, or as the prayer of confession in any communion service. After singing or reading the hymn, words of pardon and assurance should make it clear that God gives us grace, forgiveness, and a new beginning.

The early American tune is becoming more and more familiar to many congregations, and fares best with simple accompaniment. A string instrument on the melody might be the only enhancement needed. Choirs might sing a stanza in canon at one measure, but refer congregations to the text so it may be prayed.

Surely, it is God who saves me (2030)
Themes: The Christian life; canticles, choruses, and refrains; praise

"The First Song of Isaiah" is traditionally one of the lesser canticles from the Old Testament. The text comes directly from Isaiah 12:2-6 and is part of a larger prophecy that Isaiah is making regarding the fate of Israel: the Assyrians will conquer Israel but God will deliver the people and raise up from Judah a savior in whom they can put their trust. This song or "canticle" is a response to that prophecy.

The traditional position of a lesser canticle in a worship service is following the psalm and immediately after the reading of one of the "lessons" (Old or New Testament scripture appointed for the day). This song is in the form of an antiphon: a refrain followed by several stanzas of sung scripture; the refrain is sung after every stanza and then finally sung at the end. The verses (stanzas) can either be sung by a soloist, the choir, or the entire congregation.

The contemporary worship style of this setting will make the song ideal for a praise service in which multiple choruses are sung in succession. The refrain can stand on its own as a separate chorus and will be easy to memorize. Teach the refrain using a call and response method. "God" ("God's") can be substituted for "him," "he," and "his."

Swiftly pass the clouds of glory (2102)
Themes: Transfiguration; Jesus' life; God's will; light

This hymn comments on the Gospel accounts of Jesus' mountaintop Transfiguration. It is best used on Transfiguration Sunday (the Sunday before Lent begins).

The hymn tune is written in two equal parts, the first in a minor tonality, the second in a major tonality. Each half might be performed by a different group of singers or by antiphonal choirs (two choirs separated by space and singing responsively). Have the choir introduce the hymn by singing stanza 1 alone; the choir men sing the first half and the choir women sing the second half. All men of the choir and the congregation sing the first half of stanza 2, and all women sing the second half. Invite all to sing all of stanza 3. Two song leaders, a male and female, can help in leading the hymn.

Taste and see (2267)
Themes: Holy Communion; invitation

"Taste and See" is a grand and stately hymn based on the familiar verse 8 from Psalm 34 and would be ideal for use during communion. Set in a contemporary music style, this hymn has a rather long refrain with repetitive music and text. Consequently, it would be easy for most congregations to learn the refrain and sing it from memory, thus making it a natural selection when the congregation is standing, moving, or kneeling and unable to hold a hymnal or see a screen. The individual stanzas of this hymn could be sung by the choir with the congregation joining on the refrain.

Te Ofrecemos Padre Nuestro (2262)
See "Let us offer to the Father."

Thank you, Jesus (2081)
Tino Tenda, Jesu
Themes: Thanksgiving; gratitude; praise

This short Shona chorus from Zimbabwe has many potential uses in worship. It may be most appropriate when singing in response to prayers of gratitude. Another possibility is to sing it during communion.

In its original setting it would usually be sung unaccompanied except for the use of a *hosho* (a maraca-type gourd with seeds inside). A simple drum pattern might also accompany this song. The Shona people cannot stand still while singing. They often bend their knees slightly to the beat and clap. Both the drum and the clapping might emphasize the half note, creating a cross-rhythmic effect of 3/2 against 6/4. This may seem difficult for congregations, but can be easily achieved if the choir and leader are prepared. The congregation will follow by example. Don't explain it; just do it!

The Family Prayer Song (2188)
See "Come and fill our homes."

The First Song of Isaiah (2030)
See "Surely, it is God who saves me."

The Fragrance of Christ (2205)
See "Lord, may our prayer rise like incense."

The King of glory comes (2091)
Themes: Christ's triumphal entry; Second Coming; Lordship and reign

This traditional Israeli folk song is perfect for Palm Sunday. Use it as a processional complete with palm branches. The eight-bar stanza lends itself to antiphonal singing, particularly stanza 1, which is in question/answer form taken from Psalm 24. You might have a soloist sing the first four measures and the choir or congregation sing the last four measures; or, have the sopranos and altos sing the first phrase and the tenors and basses sing the second phrase. However you decide to perform this joyous song, hand claps are quite appropriate.

The Lily of the Valley (2062)
See "I have found a friend in Jesus."

The lone, wild bird (2052)

Theme: The providence and care of God

This hymn speaks of God as the Creator and sustainer of all that is in the world, from the far lands and ocean depths to a single bird in flight; and this same God knows our private thoughts, fears, hopes, and joys.

Specific stanzas might be assigned to male or female voices, and the gentle, lilting quality of the melody suggests that it might be played by a solo flute or oboe. The unity of textual and musical climax in the third phrase of each stanza suggests a louder volume at that point, although overall the hymn imparts a sense of peaceful and quiet reflection.

The nature of the melody allows it to be sung canonically (as a round), with new voices or instruments entering every two measures. This is most effectively done without keyboard accompaniment.

The Lord bless and keep you (2280)

Themes: Benediction; blessing; sending forth

This simple setting of the traditional text based on Numbers 6:24-26 is easily learned and remembered. It may be used as the benediction itself or as a congregational response to the benediction. A pulse of one beat to the measure with an unhurried tempo is effective. The second ending may be sung: "Shalom. A-men." The music should build in intensity and volume and then drop back to end softly. It may be sung a second time very softly as an "echo." It also works effectively sung in canon.

The Lord's Prayer (2278)

See "Our Father in heaven."

The Navy Hymn (2191)

See "Eternal Father, strong to save."

The Servant Song (2222)

See "Brother, sister, let me serve you."

The snow lay on the ground (2093)

Themes: Christmas Eve; Jesus' birth; angels; Mary

The scene around the manger is told in this carol. It can be sung in either a hushed, slower tempo, or in a more joyous, dancelike manner. Use it in a Lessons and Carols service during Advent, and again on Christmas Eve or Day.

The refrain in the Singer's Edition gives a lovely three-part treble harmonization that could be introduced by a women's trio or chorale. The addition of percussion instruments (triangle, finger cymbal, hand drum) can make the carol come alive.

It is fortuitous that this carol is in the same key as "O Come, All Ye Faithful" (UMH, 234) as they share the Latin refrain, "Venite adoremus Dominum." There are many ways to combine the singing of these two carols. The simplest way might be to follow the singing of 2093 with stanza 3 of "O Come, All Ye Faithful."

The Spirit sends us forth to serve (2241)

Themes: Service; Christ's call to discipleship; sending forth

This hymn contains echoes of the Magnificat and Jesus' acceptance of Isaiah's proclamation of good news to the poor and release to the captives (Luke 4:16-21). In speaking of sending forth and going, it becomes a hymn of going forth at the end of worship, as the "service" begins. Once the hymn is learned, the final stanza might be used on its own as a congregational response to the benediction. Sing it to commission youth for a work camp, volunteers for mission trips, or for a hunger walk.

The early American tune is one that is used for several hymn texts, and so may be familiar to the congregation. The flute descant might easily be added. One way to vary the singing of the entire hymn would be to have everyone sing the first and fourth verses, the women sing the second verse, and the men sing the third verse.

The Summons (2130)

See "Will you come and follow me."

The Trees of the Field (2279)

See "You shall go out with joy."

The virgin Mary had a baby boy (2098)

Themes: Christmas; Nativity; Epiphany; Incarnation

This familiar West Indian calypso can enliven worship during the Advent and Christmas season. Introduce the stanzas with a soloist or choir and invite the congregation to sing on the refrain only. A West African kind of percussion ensemble, including a shaker (maraca-type instrument or gourd with beads strung on the outside), drum, and a gong (cowbell-type sound) is also appropriate. Assign each a different pattern, creating a polyrhythmic (multilayered rhythmic texture) effect. By singing only on the refrain, worshipers can free themselves from the printed page quickly and clap, adding to the rhythmic ensemble. Use piano or guitar accompaniment.

Children will enjoy singing the stanzas. Create a live Nativity scene by adding characters in the Christmas drama on successive stanzas until it is complete. The refrain may be used separately as an acclamation or response to the Christmas Gospel readings. Substitute "Sing, Alleluia!" or "Sing, Gloria!" for "Oh, yes! believer!" in the refrain to fit the season.

There are some things I may not know (2147)
(Yes, God Is Real)
Themes: Faith; praise; witness and testimony

This testimony emphasizes the importance of feelings and emotions in spiritual encounters. It is one thing to know about God, and yet another to know God intimately by feeling God's presence and holy power deep within. This manner and depth of knowing is obviously personal but can be shared, encouraged, and expressed corporately.

This song can be used as a sung affirmation of faith. It also is an appropriate response to scriptures describing God's attributes and faithfulness.

There'll be joy in the morning (2284)
Themes: Reign of Christ; Second Coming; Advent

This hymn has an almost martial quality, but sing it with joy and expectation. It would be very appropriate on Reign of Christ/Christ the King Sunday (the Sunday before Advent begins) or during Advent. It would generally accompany any reading from the book of Revelation as well.

Sing this hymn in a bright tempo ($\downarrow$ = 100). It might be accompanied with organ, trumpet, and an improvised part for snare drum. It will be effective if the men sing stanza 1, the women sing stanza 2, and all sing stanza 3. Try singing stanza 1 again after stanza 3, but much slower and softer. While we joyfully await the reign of Christ, we must remember that it is not yet come, and that we have work to do. A slower, softer repetition of stanza 1 may musically show the longing that we have for that coming day.

There's a song (2141)
Themes: Love; peace; faith; hope; joy; gratitude

This song works well as a song of commitment, perhaps as a response to the message. Sing it in its entirety, or separate the verses from each other by a prayer or scripture reading. Find visual symbols of love, peace, faith, hope, and joy that could be shown in video, or in some live representation as a way of enhancing the congregation's connection with the song. This song also works well with children.

There's a star in the East (2096)
Themes: Christmas; Epiphany; following Jesus

The call and response structure of "Rise Up, Shepherd, and Follow" lends itself to *a cappella* singing as a choral call to worship for the choir and congregation during the season of Christmas and Epiphany. The call led by a soloist (or song leader) is followed by the response of the choir and congregation. This would also be appropriate to use with a children's choir or with combined choirs.

They'll Know We Are Christians by Our Love (2223)
See "We are one in the Spirit."

This, this is where children belong (2233)
Themes: Faith community; worship; children; family; baptism; communion

This gently flowing song welcomes children into the life of the church. It would be particularly appropriate at a baptism or communion service. It would also be effective before or after a children's message or time of prayer, or as a part of a service built around children or children's ministry.

The accompaniment should be simple, perhaps just a piano. The tempo should be approximately ♩. = 56.

This thread I weave (2185)
Themes: Social holiness; discipleship; justice ministries; commitment; the call of Christ

Lest we become too overwhelmed by the need for justice in our world, this hymn calls us to take the small steps that lead to God's peace each day. Here are things we all can do, and things that will challenge some of us, from children to carpenters, from athletes to surgeons, and on to include the heroes of the faith. Let children illustrate it, mime it, dance it, but then let grownups also take it seriously.

Use it as a response to a call to commitment to social holiness—read by different voices, sung by different voices, or in unison. Sing it after a challenge, such as "Here Am I" (2178). Have worshipers pick one phrase and write it as a pledge of commitment for a particular time period. Use it as a sermon illustration on the many ways we can serve God every day.

Thou art worthy (2041)
Themes: God's glory; God as Creator; worship of God

In this song, the congregation responds to a previously spoken or sung call to worship by singing directly to God, "Thou art worthy." Accordingly, you might use this song just before or during the offering, or just before or after a time of prayer. It might be particularly appropriate as a response to a scripture text about Creation.

This song could be quiet and meditative or loud and strong; the accompaniment could consist of a quiet guitar or piano or a majestic organ, according to the mood of the service. If you prefer, you could change the "King James" language to a more contemporary sounding "You are worthy." As written, "Thou Art Worthy" might appeal especially to those who prefer more traditional language.

Thou didst leave thy throne (2100)
Themes: Jesus' earthly life and ministry; the Christian life

This hymn was written originally intended to be sung by children. The hymn in this setting by Timothy Matthews has become popular for use during the Christmas season or Holy Week. The text gives a poetic account of Jesus' birth, life, death, and return in successive stanzas using beautiful and poignant language that will, no doubt, endear the hymn to many congregations.

In addition to being sung by the entire congregation, the carol-like language (stanza 3 mentions foxes and birds) makes the hymn ideal for use with children as it was originally intended. Teach the hymn to children. Then, try this format: first stanza, all; second stanza, women; third stanza, children; fourth stanza, men; fifth stanza, all.

Time now to gather (2265)
Theme: Holy Communion

It is sometimes from the most basic, simple elements that the most profound creations come, and such is this hymn. What is communion? It is gathering, Christ's presence, a meal of grain and fruit, remembrance, thanksgiving, welcome, feeding the hungry, healing the hurting. This simple recalling of the most basic elements of communion is this text's beauty. The entire melody is made of only two rhythmic units, and these units are repeated in each line. Each of the four phrases is made of only repeated notes and short motives that move by step. This simplicity of music and directness of text combine in great beauty to form a hymn that congregations will sing well even the very first time, and will want to sing again and again.

If it is desired that this hymn be sung by soloists, it provides an opportunity to effectively use many different singers, each one singing one or two of the short phrases or component ideas. Choir members will easily be able to improvise a harmony part at the interval of a third or sixth below the melody.

Tino Tenda, Jesu (2081)
See "Thank you, Jesus."

To know you in all of your glory (2161)

Themes: Knowing God; prayer; God's glory, power, and mercy; love for God

Expressing an earnest desire to know, love, trust, and serve God, this song could be effective before the scripture is read, before or after the sermon, or before or after a time of prayer. Prayers by congregation members or a worship leader could be spoken between the stanzas, expanding on each stanza's message.

With a somewhat slow tempo (about ♩. = 82), some percussion will help to hold this song together. The accompaniment should emphasize beats 1 and 7, with the stronger emphasis on beat 1. Piano and guitars will work well for this song.

To Know You More (2161)

See "To know you in all of your glory."

Together we serve (2175)

Themes: Social holiness; community; outreach and witnessing; missions

Many church communities today have diverse congregations made up of people from different cultures, backgrounds, and experiences. This simple and beautiful hymn by Daniel Charles Damon leads the singer to a fuller understanding of community and how people can work together through love to create an inviting climate where all will be welcome.

Teach the tune by using call and response: the song leader sings a phrase and then the congregation answers back. The simplicity of the tune reflects the simple message of the text. Also, the direction for the congregation to sing in unison is a powerful metaphor for the unity that the hymn proclaims.

Use this hymn whenever there is an emphasis on outreach and witnessing. In addition, there are often opportunities to end a service by reinforcing the concept of community within the congregation. This hymn would be a great substitute for such hymns as "Blest Be the Tie That Binds" (UMH, 557).

Tuya Es la Gloria (2011)

See "We sing of your glory."

Two fishermen (2101)

Themes: Jesus' call; discipleship; ministry in daily life

Like the disciples, we are called by Jesus to acts of ministry. This hymn is appropriate for any worship service that calls us into service. The Gospel accounts upon which the hymn is based appear following Epiphany in each year of the lectionary. Sing the hymn following the reading of these Gospel lessons.

The entire hymn melody can be accompanied by the open fifth found in the first measure of the bass clef accompaniment. Use only these two notes played on the organ or handbells for a minimal accompaniment of stanza 1.

Though not noted, the melody can serve as a round, with part 2 entering one measure after part 1. Keep the "drone" accompaniment from stanza 1 and add a flute playing part 2 of the round to accompany stanza 2.

The fourth stanza and the refrain can be used as a fitting response to the benediction. The choir might continually repeat the last two measures as they leave the worship space, showing that Christ's call continues on and on.

Ubi Caritas (2179)
See "Live in charity."

Unsettled world (2183)

Themes: Grace; world peace; judgment; the city; daily work; penitence; Kingdom of God; call to prayer; confession

"Unsettled World" is a hymn that laments the hectic and impersonal pace of the modern world. The contradictions and unfairness of life are highlighted as the hymn calls the singer to approach God for peace. The hymn is essentially a call for a community of faith in the midst of a milieu that defies community.

Hal Hopson's tune, THUNDER BAY, is a simple melody with repetitive figures, making it relatively easy for congregations to learn. The transparent accompaniment complements the call of the text for peace in the midst of turbulence. Appropriate uses for this hymn would be in any service that deals with the hectic pace of modern life. The serene nature of the text and tune also lends itself as a call to prayer or even a call to confession.

Uyai Mose (2274)
See "Come, all you people."

Vengan Todos Adoremos (2271)
See "Come! Come! Everybody worship."

Veni Sancte Spiritus (2118)
See "Holy Spirit, come to us."

Victim Divine (2259)

Themes: Holy Communion; Jesus as our great High Priest; salvation; sacrifice; God's love; blood of Christ

This hymn carries many images of the Lord's Supper as a means of grace as understood by the Wesleys. Christ is the sacrifice made for us, as spoken of in Hebrews 10:12-22. He stands in the Holy of Holies, giving us salvation with his blood. As the smoke of Christ's offering rises, God calls us sinners to inherit a crown. And through Christ's offering of himself we are given life, joy, and peace. The final stanza reminds us that we do not need to "go up to heaven" to bring Christ down; here he is in communion, here at the table he meets us in love.

Give the tune the majestic tempo the text demands, paced to let the text be understood, but still with a sense of deep joy. The final stanza might be used as an choral call to worship on Communion Sundays.

Wa Wa Wa Emimimo (2124)
See "Come, O Holy Spirit, come."

Wade in the water (2107)
Themes: The grace of God in salvation; deliverance; baptism; healing

The dual reminder of God's power in the midst of calm waters as well as in troubled or stirred waters sets the momentum for the cadence of this spiritual. The initial biblical setting of troubled waters (John 5:2-9) provides the imagery of the pool by the Sheep Gate (called Bethzatha in Hebrew), which produces healing when the water is stirred. The spiritual also evokes memories of God's saving grace in the Red Sea passage (stanzas 1-2), and looks forward with hope to God's continuous acts of healing, saving, and deliverance (stanzas 3-4). This song can be used as part of baptismal and healing services, and during any service following the reading of John 5:2-9 or Exodus 14:21-31. A moderately slow and steady unaccompanied vocal tempo should be maintained throughout. If accompaniment is used it should be controlled so that the congregation does not increase the tempo.

Walk with me (2242)
Themes: Commitment; unity; community

This swinging, gospel song is a good song of commitment, and would fit a theme of community and mission. It can be used to tie into the subject of journeying and of trying to understand God's vision for our individual lives. Sing this song congregationally, with accompaniment, or present this song as special music, with either a very small group singing it, or the choir singing it *a cappella*. Suggested tempo: (♩ = 84).

Water, River, Spirit, Grace (2253)
Themes: Baptismal covenant; renewal; prayer; contemporary praise and prayer

Thomas Troeger's gift for using symbolic language effectively is clearly manifest in this song. It can be used to introduce or conclude a time of prayer. In services of renewal of the baptismal covenant, it can be sung over and over again (in Taizé style) as members of the congregation come forward to renew their baptismal covenant. It can also be used in a contemporary service with creative accompaniment by an instrumental ensemble. It will rapidly become a beloved tradition for congregations who use it.

In introducing the tune, one could have a solo voice sing the melody line through once, with the choir and then the congregation joining in. Observe the rhythm of "the depths your finger traced"—it is not what one expects! This melody "carries the words" especially well. Sing it until the song sings you.

We all are one in mission (2243)
Themes: The nature of the church; mission of the church; gifts and talents; community
Rusty Edwards's hymn, "We all are one in mission," is based on 1 Corinthians 12:4-6 and is a marvelous exposition of the concept of diverse gifts and ministries, but of one Lord who activates them in everyone. Although individuals within a church community may possess various talents and abilities, all work together for the common good united by Jesus Christ.

The tune, KOURTANE (also called NYLAND), is a Finnish folk melody that most congregations will find easy to learn and fun to sing. It consists of four musical phrases, three of which are almost identical. If the octave leap toward the end of the last phrase proves to be problematic, then sing the last phrase exactly like the second phrase.

Use this hymn whenever there is a need to draw the community together. If "Blest Be the Tie That Binds" (UMH, 557) has been overused, then this hymn would be a perfect substitute.

We Are Called (2172)
See "Come! Live in the light!"

We are God's people (2220)
Themes: The church; community of faith; Body of Christ; unity
This is a hymn about the church as God's people, the Bride of Christ, the Body of Christ, and the Spirit's dwelling place. In addition to the scriptures listed with the hymn, it is also appropriate for Pentecost (the birthday of the church), for church homecomings, church dedications, and ecumenical services. It would make a good study hymn for a class on the church and its many scriptural images, either for confirmation or adult classes.

The beginning of the melody may be familiar to some as one of the lyric melodies from a symphony by Johannes Brahms. The ending may be less familiar, so make certain that it is included in the introduction. A French horn or trumpet may help to reinforce the melody. Strong unison singing will reinforce the unity mentioned in the text.

We are marching in the light of God (2235-b)
Siyahamba/Caminando
Themes: Hope; assurance; perseverance

"Siyahamba" is a freedom song from South Africa in a Zulu/Xhosa dialect. These are two of the major languages in South Africa. "We" signifies the importance of community. "Marching" indicates that the community must respond actively, even in the face of oppression. "Light of God" is a figure of speech that indicates the direction of the march, and that God has provided a path even under the most difficult of circumstances. Sing this song as a pro-cessional—a common practice with African choirs. It could also be sung as a congregation leaves the church following worship to return to the world.

"Siyahamba" should always be sung with swaying. African music almost always demands a physical response. Drums do not play as great a role in the music of southern Africa as in other parts of the continent. Light drumming is possible, but not at all necessary for this selection to be effective. More impor-tant is to sing unaccompanied, if possible. The Spanish text is also an effective variation when repeating the song several times. Although not indicated in the score, it would be common for the leader to sing over the end of phrases (dotted half notes) by anticipating the text to follow. Keep the beat steady and do not slow down until the final cadence.

This arrangement (2235-b) includes the original Zulu language. See "We are singing for the Lord is our light" (2235-a) for phonetic syllables and alter-nate text.

We are one in Christ Jesus (2229)
Somos Uno en Cristo
Themes: Unity; the Body of Christ

The text for this Latin American song is based on Ephesians 4:4-6—there is one Spirit and one body—the Body of Christ. It is an example of a *corito* or *estri-billo*—a short refrain that has a specific place in Hispanic worship. This partic-ular corito can be used to gather the community for worship, as a response to the Word, as a song of affirmation of faith, or as a song of praise. It is very appropriate for Worldwide Communion Sunday, and for services during the Week of Prayer for Christian Unity held in January.

It might be helpful for the congregation to learn the tune first, using a syl-lable such as "lah." Encourage them to sing the song in Spanish. If this is too difficult, let them sing only the first part in Spanish. The leader will introduce it, then the congregation will repeat.

This works well with guitar accompaniment at a moderate tempo ($\quarternote$ = 96-112). Other instruments could include:

Claves:

A common pattern in Hispanic congregational singing is hand clapping. With this particular song, one would normally clap on every beat, with an occasional variation at the end of phrases, or at the end of the piece:

last time

We are one in the Spirit (2223)
Themes: Unity; ministry in daily life; praise; commitment
This chorus will already be familiar to many worshipers. It works especially well as a response to the Word and as a sending forth to be God's people. It also serves as a call to show God's love to others by being in service to them.

Add some variety to this song by using conga drums or a strong bass drum, along with guitar, electric bass, and tambourine. One possible use of this song may be around the time of July 4. Consider a visual representation of life in America, showing all different aspects of relationships—both positive and negative, both healthy and fractured. It would raise the question about whether or not our nation was "one nation under God," and would give an opportunity to talk about the changing culture in which we live, where the majority of people are not Christians. Another way to use this song would be to think of all the ways in which Jesus' love pulls people together, sharing a slide show of people in relationship with one another and in service to the world, including people of all ages, races, and ethnicity.

We are singing for the Lord is our light (2235a)
Siyahamba/Caminando
See "We are marching in the light of God" (2235b) for commentary. This arrangement of "Siyahamba" (2235a) includes phonetic syllables for the original Zulu language. It also provides an alternate text and arrangement.

We are standing on holy ground (2272)
Themes: Adoration and praise; holiness; God's presence
The author/composer wrote this song at age nineteen for the first service to be held in his congregation's new sanctuary. His father, the pastor, had requested that he write a special song for the service. When Geron Davis asked

himself the question, "What do we want to say when we come into this place for the first time," the answer came quickly in the form of a powerful song that moves worshipers into God's presence.

A worship sequence might begin with "Holy Ground" by Christopher Beatty and move immediately, building in intensity, to Davis's "Holy Ground." The modulation from E♭ major to F major (Singer's/Accompaniment Editions) builds to a powerful climax. The depth of meaning in this song will be even more powerful if it is visually interpreted by dance because when we are in God's presence, we are truly on holy ground.

This song is especially appropriate to use with the scripture story of Moses encountering the burning bush (Exod. 3:1-6).

We Are the Body of Christ (2227)
See "One heart, one spirit."

We bring the sacrifice of praise (2031)
Themes: Praise and thanksgiving; adoration

This is a high-energy song (♩ = 108-120) most often used as an opening to the worship service. Scripture has instructed us that bringing our praises is the very prerequisite to knowing God's presence. Therefore, a nice way to begin a service is by reading Psalm 107:22 or Hebrews 13:15 during the instrumental introduction to this song. Then sing the first two phrases in unison and begin harmony on the third phrase, "And we offer up to you."

This is a contemporary song that works well in combination with traditional hymns. Two possibilities are "Holy, Holy, Holy! Lord God Almighty" (NICAEA) and "All Creatures of Our God and King" (LASST UNS ERFREUEN). A possible opening worship medley could be: "He Has Made Me Glad" (2270); "We Bring the Sacrifice of Praise" (D major only); "Holy, Holy, Holy! Lord God Almighty" (UMH, 64); and "I Will Call upon the Lord" (2002).

We gather here in Jesus' name (2269)
Themes: Holy Communion; family of Christ; forgiveness; presence of Christ; anticipation of heaven; Second Coming

This beautiful communion song has five stanzas. Each is important, so it is best to sing the song as a whole. The lines "Come, take the bread; come, drink the wine; come, share the Lord" are repeated in stanzas 1, 3, and 5. Even when hearing it for the first time, the congregation should be able to sing these repeated lines. A choir or ensemble could sing the song, inviting the congregation to follow and join as they learn the melody. Perhaps the best place for this song would be as the invitation to communion, after the Great Thanksgiving but before the sharing of the bread and cup. It could also be sung as the congregation comes forward to receive communion.

Keyboard and/or guitar accompaniment would work well. The song should be performed freely and expressively, at a tempo around 68-72 beats per minute.

We have come at Christ's own bidding (2103)
Themes: Transfiguration; Jesus' life; opening of worship

The text of this hymn helps us to identify with the feelings of the disciples as they saw Jesus transfigured in front of them. Use this hymn on Transfiguration Sunday (the Sunday before Lent begins).

This familiar hymn tune (HYFRYDOL) makes the text very accessible to congregational singers. Intersperse the stanzas of the hymn through the Gospel reading on Transfiguration Sunday. Sing stanza 1 before the reading and stanza 3 after the reading. Find an appropriate place in the Gospel reading to sing stanza 2.

The hymn stanzas might also be used throughout the worship service, either by the choir or by the entire congregation. Stanza 1 is a great call to worship. Stanza 2 can accompany the Gospel reading. Finally, stanza 3 can serve as a benediction response.

We need a faith (2181)
Themes: Grace; faith; community; trust; race relations; cultural diversity; daily work

Any gathering that accentuates the commonality within a diverse community will find this hymn particularly appropriate. A service commemorating Martin Luther King, Jr., Day is generally an opportunity to highlight race relations and ethnic/cultural diversity. This hymn would be a perfect selection for such a service.

The tune, CRIMOND, is probably familiar as "The Lord's My Shepherd, I'll Not Want" (UMH, 136). Sing the hymn slowly but robustly and in unison on the first and last stanzas. If parts are used, try singing *a cappella*.

We sang our glad hosannas (2111)
Themes: Palm Sunday; Easter; communion

A moderate tempo is best for this hymn ($\downarrow$ = 108). When introducing the hymn you might use a children's choir to sing stanza 1. Ask the choir to sing the alternate choral setting of stanza 2 in the Accompaniment and Singer's Editions. A small group might sing stanza 3, while the choir and congregation sing stanza 4. If the hymn is more familiar and all are singing all four stanzas, you might try to imperceptibly slow the tempo and decrease the volume as you move through the stanzas, ending stanza 4 in an emotional, almost whispered, "why!"

The stanzas can also be sung either during the lengthy Gospel reading on Palm/Passion Sunday or during the appropriate services of Holy Week.

Stanzas 1-2 are sung on Palm Sunday, stanza 3 on Holy Thursday, stanza 4 on Good Friday. Use stanza 5 as a call to worship on Easter Sunday.

We sing of your glory (2011)
Tuya Es la Gloria
Themes: Praise; God's dominion over Creation

This beautiful traditional song from Latin America focuses on God's grandeur and magnificence. All power, all glory belong to God. The Spanish text in the second stanza speaks of surrender not only of our whole being, but also a surrender of thrones and principalities. All surrender to God.

This is basically a song of praise that can be used as an opening hymn. Stanzas 1 and 2 could serve as a call to worship, sung either by the choir *a cappella* or by the congregation. These two stanzas could also be read, with the leader reading the first part and the congregation answering "for you are eternal. Amen. Amen."

The third stanza could be used as a response to an altar call, to be sung either before or after the pastoral prayer. The fourth stanza could serve as a sung response to the Gospel lessons during the Advent/Christmas seasons.

Keyboard and flute work well with this piece. Suggested tempo: ($\quartnote$ = 108).

We sing to you, O God (2001)
Themes: Praise of God; God's care, protection, and leading

Following a rousing opening stanza of praise to God, this hymn presents images of God as one who protects, shelters, and guides us as we live out our lives, even in the times when we wander into uncertainty, fear, or danger. The text's themes and images are related to scripture texts in Exodus 19:4; Isaiah 40:28-31; and especially Deuteronomy 32:10-13. This hymn can serve well with others in *The United Methodist Hymnal* with similar themes, including "How Like a Gentle Spirit" (115); "The Care the Eagle Gives Her Young" (118); "Children of the Heavenly Father" (141); and "On Eagle's Wings" (143). These hymns, however, all are set to rather quiet and meditative musical settings, while "We Sing to You, O God" is set to the stirring DARWALL'S 148th tune. It could be used as an opening or closing hymn of praise.

Other occasions when this hymn might be used include those that recognize or celebrate our journey through life: church anniversary, marking the secular New Year, or a time of conflict or loss.

We walk by faith (2196)
Themes: Faith; turning doubt to belief

This hymn recognizes that we, like all Christians before us who were not firsthand witnesses to Christ's Resurrection, have come to belief through faith, and through our faith to the assurance that we have been claimed by God forever. Unlike Thomas, we cannot touch the wounds of the crucified Christ, and yet it is our desire to believe.

The MARTYRDOM tune is used for the quiet hymn, "Alas! and Did My Savior Bleed" (UMH, 294), often sung on Good Friday. This, however, is not a quiet, meditative hymn; rather, it is a hymn to be sung with strength and conviction, and should be so accompanied. The repetition of the opening stanza to conclude the hymn is not whimsy, and should not be omitted. It brings us back to the reality of our present earthly existence, and reminds us that for now, our faith is sufficient.

An alternate organ harmonization is included in the Accompaniment Edition.

We were baptized in Christ Jesus (2251)
Themes: The sacraments; baptism; confirmation; reaffirmation

Stanza 1 of this hymn speaks mainly of the sacrament of baptism and of our being united with God. Stanza 2 includes baptism, along with communion and the welcoming of the risen Christ as a new beginning, marking a change in direction, perhaps signified by the rite of confirmation or reaffirmation. Either of these two stanzas, or both together could be used on occasions when any of these rites were celebrated. The third stanza is an ascription of praise to the Trinity using the familiar words of the Gloria Patri, and it could be sung separately in a service in place of one of the other Gloria Patris in the hymnal, or as a doxology.

As a hymn that celebrates new beginnings and the sacraments, it should be sung joyously and with strength, especially when concluded by the third stanza's Gloria Patri. It is most appropriate sung by the entire congregation, symbolic of the welcome, love, and support extended to those newly baptized or confirmed.

We will glorify the King of kings (2087)
Themes: Adoration and praise of Jesus; Jesus' Lordship and reign

This majestic contemporary chorus is musically repetitious, but in four stanzas gives a complete picture of who Jesus is. Vary the way it is sung so the melodic repetition is interesting. One possibility is to sing the first stanza in solo phrases, the second stanza with everyone in unison, the third stanza in parts, and then modulate up for the final stanza with the descant.

Stanzas 1 and 4 are appropriate for Palm Sunday when combined with other songs for the day. If used on Christ the King Sunday, combine with "All Hail King Jesus" (2069) and "O Worship the King" (UMH, 73). The tempo and style should be majestic and strong ($\quarternote$ = 82).

What a mighty God we serve (2021)
Theme: Acclamation of praise

This very powerful affirmation and response, simply expressed is very appropriate after the confession and pardon and sermons that focus on the mighty acts of God. Like other straightforward and repetitious musical statements, this one takes on new life with the addition of ways to praise the Lord other than those listed. Add additional stanzas, such as "let us dance and praise the Lord," "let us clap," and "let us serve."

What a wonderful change (2140)
Theme: Rebirth and a new life in Christ

This song is the personal testimony of one whose life has been radically changed by an encounter with Jesus. As either a solo or a congregational testimony song, its natural setting is a service with an evangelistic emphasis. It can be part of an opening praise service. It can follow preaching on personal rebirth and new life in Christ. It can lead people into a spirit of prayer and meditation, when paired with "Into My Heart" (2160). It can reawaken faith and fervor in older persons who remember this song from their youth. It is fun to sing, expressing the joy of the Christian life. Singing in parts, especially the refrain, makes this song even more joyful.

Careful observance of the fermatas, strategically placed to divide the hymn's stanzas from its refrain, not only marks the hymn's form but also provides the singers with a natural place to breathe and a brief respite from the rushing forward motion. The melodic line's rise of an octave plus two notes in the final two lines, culminating on the final fermata, provides one of the great climactic moments in all of gospel hymnody.

What does the Lord require of you (2174)
Themes: Justice; holiness; mercy; thanksgiving

This setting of the text from Micah can be easily taught and repeated endlessly. Begin by teaching the basses their part. As they continue to sing, add the alto and tenor part (note that this part is sung on a unison note, not in octaves). Finally add the soprano part.

If the song is known, use it with a reading of Micah 6:6-8. Have everyone sing the bass part. Keep repeating this while a reader reads the Micah passage. After the reading, add the alto/tenor and soprano parts. Accompany simply with guitar or piano. Other instruments might play the vocal parts as they enter. The chord progression of this song is very similar to the popular Pachelbel's Canon in D. You might be creative in combining the two.

When Cain killed Abel (2135)

Themes: The Christian life; community; reconciliation; social concerns; trust; penitence

"When Cain Killed Abel" is a hymn that expresses deep sentiments that are eventually experienced by every person, family, and community. Strong emotions, such as jealousy, rivalry, and hatred can sometimes damage relationships almost beyond repair. This hymn compares the stories of great biblical characters (Cain and Abel, Jacob and Joseph) to the experiences of modern Christians. This hymn would be appropriately used in any situation in which human relationships are examined, such as services of personal or community healing or services of penance (Ash Wednesday, Lent).

The tune, AFTER THE FALL, is in a minor mode and expresses the seriousness of situations in which human relationships are strained. The hymn should be sung in a slow and stately manner. Individual stanzas could be sung by different groups; for example, women could sing stanza 2; men could sing stanza 3.

This hymn would also be appropriate for private devotion for an individual who is struggling with these strong emotions. Read the text through one stanza at a time, pausing briefly to meditate or pray before continuing with the next stanza.

When God restored our common life (2182)

Themes: Grace; faith; community; trust; reconciliation; justice; missions; witnessing

This beautiful hymn by Ruth Duck is a paraphrase of Psalm 126 and would be appropriate to be sung when the lectionary calls for this psalm. The imagery depicted in the text lends itself to many possible situations, such as community life, sowing seeds of faith, working with joy, liberating oppressed people, righteousness and justice, and praying for those who suffer wrongly.

The tune, RESIGNATION, is a popular American folk tune with a pentatonic flavor. Consequently, singing the tune unaccompanied and in unison would add a rustic quality, which could help highlight the meaning of the text. Nevertheless, the harmonization is very beautiful and the hymn should also be sung in parts if possible. Try singing the first and third stanzas in unison with a simple organ registration (or piano alone), and sing the second stanza *a cappella* in parts (or choir alone). For the adventurous, try singing the hymn in unison as a two-part round with the second part entering on the third beat of the first full measure. However the hymn is sung, it should not be rushed but should be sung slowly and with dignity.

When Jesus wept (2106)

Themes: Jesus' passion; Lent

This canon is by early American composer William Billings. It will be familiar to many with choral experience because it has most often been used as a choir anthem rather than a congregational hymn. The text speaks of Christ's suffering: the tears of Jesus show his great compassion for all humanity; his pain and suffering shames humanity for rejecting him.

This song is appropriate during the season of Lent, especially during Holy Week, when the events in Jesus' life lead him to crucifixion. The vocal range of this song is rather wide, and there are a few tricky intervals for the singers. Use the choir to introduce this song, and make sure most of the choir sings with the congregation. Use a few strong singers in canon with the congregation. Place them on the sides and behind the congregation when the congregation is confident of its own part. This song is best sung unaccompanied. If accompaniment is used, a single instrument to reinforce the melody is most appropriate.

When we are called to sing your praise (2216)

Themes: Grace; comfort in the midst of adversity and loss; grief; funerals and memorial services

Mary Nelson Keithahn's hymn is a song of praise in the midst of adversity and loss. Congregations will no doubt find the language of the hymn refreshing, for example, "we would rather sit and weep or stand up to complain." The hymn would be most appropriately used in a service dealing with loss and grief, such as a funeral service.

Ralph Vaughan Williams's tune, KINGSFOLD, is a popular tune beloved by many congregations. Because of its folklike character and "snappy" rhythm, it is often sung too fast. The meter in this setting has been changed from that of "O Sing a Song of Bethlehem" (UMH, 179) to a meter more suggestive of a slower pace. Sing this hymn slowly and with dignity.

Where Children Belong (2233)

See "This, this is where children belong."

Where the Spirit of the Lord is (2119)

Themes: Holy Spirit; peace; love; help and comfort; light in darkness

This song reminds the congregation of the peace, love, comfort, and power we can find in the presence of God, no matter what our circumstances. It would be especially appropriate in helping the congregation respond to a death or other difficult time or "darkness." It is also a good song to sing before, after, or during a time of prayer. This song would also be good on a Sunday when the scripture for the day has to do with the Holy Spirit, such as Pentecost Sunday. Another use for this song would be in a wedding ceremony, as a reminder of the importance of the presence of God in the marriage and in the home.

Piano, organ, and/or guitar(s) could accompany this song effectively. A tempo around $\quarternote = 96$ would work well.

Who is my mother, who is my brother? (2225)
Themes: Communion; unity; brokenness; family of God; service

In the brokenness of the world, Christ gives us unity. This beautiful text is appropriate anytime the worship service deals with service to others, celebrating diversity and unity, or witnessing to the open invitation to the communion table. It would be very appropriate on Holy Thursday or at any other celebration of communion.

This hymn can be accompanied with organ, piano, or guitar, but any accompaniment should always be simple. The tempo should be about ♩ = 120.

The hymn may be sung as an invitation to communion, either before or after the Prayer of Great Thanksgiving. A soloist and the congregation can easily alternate singing the lines of the hymn. This would be especially appropriate if the soloist were the clergyperson celebrating communion. The celebrant sings/asks the first line's question and the congregation responds by singing the second line answer. This alternation can continue through the entire hymn.

Why has God forsaken me? (2110)
Themes: Holy Week; Good Friday; love; mystery of faith; the Crucifixion

This poignant hymn uses a Japanese pentatonic scale (D, E, F, A, B, with E as the home tone) as the basis of the melody. The text is by New Zealander, William Wallace. Try this tune without any harmonization. Much Asian music needs no additional harmony. Accompany only with a flute or oboe. The use of a single instrument symbolizes how alone Christ felt upon the cross.

This song draws on Christ's words on the cross, "My God, my God, why have you forsaken me?" (Matt. 27:46). It is most appropriate during Holy Week. This hymn could follow a Good Friday sermon. Another possibility is to design a hymn and prayer service around Christ's seven last words drawn from the Gospels. This hymn might also frame a time of prayer or silent meditation. Sing the first two stanzas before the prayer or silence and the final two stanzas following the prayer or silence. It would be appropriate to sing during a Maundy Thursday communion.

Why should I feel discouraged? (2146)
Themes: God's grace and providential care; assurance

Many older persons remember Ethel Waters singing this song as her personal testimony in numerous Billy Graham crusades. Her signature song in earlier years had been "Stormy Weather," but Jesus had changed her life and she entitled her autobiography *His Eye Is on the Sparrow*. Sung as a solo or by a congregation, this song is the testimony of all those whose life has been full of stormy weather but whose friendship with Jesus has made them happy and free. Jesus in this song is not a distant ruler, but a friend who stands by our side through every trouble. It is a song of invitation for persons who need such a Jesus. It is an invitation for older persons to remember when they heard this

118

song many years ago and to reawaken their first youthful love of Jesus. As such, it can be part of an opening praise service or follow preaching on these themes.

Many soloists sing this song with a slower, more deliberate tempo at the beginning, appropriate to the text of the verses. They set a quicker tempo in keeping with the joy expressed by the refrain, and then return to the slower style to conclude the song. Many congregations will take delight in being offered the opportunity to employ this variety of expression.

Why stand so far away, my God (2180)
Themes: Suffering; justice; lament; social holiness

This contemporary text reflects the great laments found in the Psalms. It was written to express solidarity with oppressed peoples suffering from injustice. This hymn can be used whenever the lectionary readings refer to times of injustice (e.g., bondage in Egypt, the Babylonian Captivity). It speaks powerfully to the contemporary situation as well, and can give voice to our questions and commitments in the face of injustice today.

Let the music communicate the plaintive cry of lament in the first three stanzas, building in volume and intensity on the last two stanzas. The first three stanzas could be sung by solo voices, with the choir singing the fourth stanza, and the congregation joining in the prayer and commitment of the fifth.

Wild and lone the prophet's voice (2089)
Themes: Baptism of Jesus Christ; John the Baptizer; repentance; baptism; Lamb of God; discipleship

This hymn is a powerful statement about the meaning of our baptism and the baptism of Jesus Christ in the Jordan by John the Baptizer. Following the Gospels, it is a clear call to discipleship, repentance, and justice. Sing it for the Sunday of the Baptism of the Lord (after Epiphany in early January), during Lent, when John appears in the Advent scriptures, and for any time of baptism, confirmation, or baptismal reaffirmation.

Two persons could sing this hymn as a narrator and the voice of John the Baptizer (the parts in quotations, from the middle of stanza 1 through the end of stanza 2). The congregation might join in the final lines of the third stanza, "So we dare to journey on." Doubling the melody on a reed instrument will help its learning.

Will you come and follow me (2130)
Themes: Ministry in daily life; God's call to us; service to others; commitment; commissioning to a particular act of ministry

This dancelike hymn comes from the Iona Community in Scotland. The first four verses ("will you come and follow me") are spoken from God to us in a variety of ministry settings with all kinds of people. The last verse is our response to God. Because of this structure, one way to sing this hymn is to have the first four verses sung by a song leader or other soloist, choir, or small ensemble. The last verse may be sung by the congregation as an act of response to God's call.

This hymn is especially appropriate as a response to the Word, a closing hymn, or other response. The tempo of this song is lively ($\downarrow$. = 80).

Within the day-to-day (2245)
Themes: Christian service; ministry of all believers

Subtitled "A Hymn for Deacons," this hymn is a celebration of the acts of ministry all believers can do in the everyday activities of life. Without taking away from the accomplishments of specialists such as artists, surgeons, and plumbers, new hope and miracles are also to be found in the simple gifts made by children's hands and in the little acts of caring and compassion extended to one another by ordinary people. God places equal value on all gifts and all ministries. Children will enjoy learning and singing this hymn because it recognizes and values their gifts; and twenty-first-century adults who still measure their self-worth by the importance of their vocations will also be affirmed. This hymn would be appropriate on Labor Day Sunday or in any Sunday of commissioning for service or dedication of talents.

The many melodic leaps will not be a problem for most congregations, but extra attention to the differences between the first and second endings might be required. The percussive quality of a handbell choir doubling the melody an octave higher will help in learning this hymn.

Without seeing you (2206)
Themes: Trust; faith; hope in Christ

The believer's relationship to God comes not through physical human senses, but through personal experience and emotion. Thus, we love without seeing; we embrace without touching; we follow without knowing; and we believe without seeing. This is not prayer of petition or repentance. It is a joyous affirmation of faith.

The return of the opening refrain following each verse suggests a dividing of the verses into men's and women's voices, or song leader and congregation, with the choir singing the third stanza. The familiar words of Psalm 23 in verse 4 should be sung by all, leading to a joyous final refrain.

Woke Up This Morning (2082)
See "Oh, I woke up this morning."

Womb of life, and source of being (2046)
Themes: The Trinity as a model for life in community; Holy Communion

Ruth Duck blends metaphors (both old and new) in this Trinitarian hymn, which has phrases that relate to Christmas ("Word in flesh"); Easter ("Life of Life, and Death of Death, Risen Christ"); Pentecost ("Brooding Spirit"); and Trinity Sunday ("Father, Spirit, Only Son"). Appropriate for use at any service of Holy Communion, it enriches Eucharistic celebrations with scriptural allusions to Genesis 1:1-2; Psalm 23; John 1:14, 14:26, 20:19-23; and Hebrews 5:1-10. Those who are themselves struggling with memory loss, or who have a friend or relative with that experience will find the prayer in the third stanza particularly poignant, but for churches too often beset by "spiritual amnesia" the text has a much wider connotation.

An effective introduction to the hymn may be provided by having the melody line played by an unaccompanied solo instrument (for example, a flute, oboe, or violin). Note the unexpected musical conclusion in the last two measures and prepare the song leader or choir in advance. The melody is easy to sing, but having a soloist or the choir (singing the melody line in unison) on the first stanza will help the congregation learn the tune.

Wonder of wonders, here revealed (2247)
Themes: Sacraments of the church; baptism of a child; confirmation of a child

This hymn by Jane Parker Huber is a unique hymn for the special occasion of the baptism or confirmation of a child. The melodic range of the tune, PENTECOST, by William Boyd is very limited (augmented 5th) and consists almost entirely of stepwise motion. Consequently, most congregations will find it easy to learn with little or no preparation. Sing the hymn either in unison or parts.

Would I have answered when you called (2137)
Theme: Answering the call of Christ

Of the many hymns that use the theme of responding to the call to follow Christ in a life of ministry and service, this one may be unique in expressing the doubt and hesitancy felt by the one called. After voicing those probing questions, the hymn concludes with a prayer for strength to overcome those doubts and follow.

This hymn may find favor with young people who so often experience such feelings of doubt and inadequacy, but who may be seeking meaning and direction in their lives. It is certainly appropriate for youth meetings, retreats, and summer camps. It is also appropriate for many middle-aged and mature adults whose life circumstances present them with a second or even third career, or who may be seeking new meaning and direction in their lives within the church.

The KINGSFORD tune is often used with joyous and celebratory texts. Its use with this text calls for a slower, more reflective tempo. There is a vocal descant in the Accompaniment Edition that can also be doubled on an instrument.

Wounded world that cries for healing (2177)
Themes: Social healing; world compassion; justice

This text is filled with words and phrases that will have immediate impact on many contemporary worshipers: "wounded systems," "dollars ration out compassion," "nation's spent frustration," and "tax and tithe are for a purpose." It recognizes that governments and agencies outside the church also bear a responsibility for social justice and the common good, while inside the church our prayer is, "Jesus of the healing Spirit, free us to another way!"

Instrumentalists introducing this tune to the congregation for the first time might consider playing it through in unison or octave melody so the singers can hear the wide leaps and at times disjunct melody. Organists would aid the congregation with a strong solo melody while accompanying the first stanza, or perhaps having a solo trumpet double the melody.

Yes, God Is Real (2147)
See "There are some things I may not know."

You alone are holy (2077)
Sólo Tú Eres Santo
Theme: The holiness of God

This wonderful text and beautiful melody from Latin America invite us to enter into an attitude of prayer and offer homage to God. It should be sung at a relaxed, nonrestrictive tempo, allowing the congregation to enter into communion with God through the song. It may be used as an opening hymn of praise, as a response to prayer or to the Word.

By way of introduction, have a flute soloist play one verse, with or without keyboard accompaniment, then have the congregation join in the singing. It is particularly appropriate for Transfiguration Sunday, during the Easter Season and for Pentecost Day.

Guitar accompaniment is very appropriate for this piece. Also, the use of maracas will give the song more of a Latin flavor. Play the maracas using a downward motion from the wrist only.

Suggested tempo: ($\downarrow$ = 92).

You Are Mine (2218)
See "I will come to you in the silence."

You are my hiding place (2055)

Themes: Lent; trust in God; assurance; God's providential care

This song has a haunting melody, and the content is meditative and lamenting. Use it during the Lenten season, with only guitar to accompany the congregation, and/or a well-played violin. Another idea would be to use this song through the Lenten series every week for a specific part of the service, such as the Prayers of the People. Although it might be tempting to resolve the final cadence with a major chord, keeping it in the minor tonality adds to the mysterious aspect of this song.

You are salt for the earth (2190)

Themes: Parables of Jesus; life of Jesus; Kingdom of God

This song is very fitting during the season after Epiphany. Accompany it with guitar, piano, and percussion. The tempo should move along ($\quarternote = 72$). Be sure the leader is a strong, vibrant singer who will engage the congregation and invite them to sing. On the last verse, invite the congregation to sing the entire verse rather than the call and response of the previous verses.

On the refrain add slight crescendo through the second, fourth, sixth, and eighth measures, making the words "mercy," "peace," "justice," and "God" the loudest. Invite the singers to add to their praise with hand claps on the refrain. In a more informal setting, you might divide the singers into three groups. Group 1 sings the first phrase of the refrain, group 2 sings the second phrase, group 3 sings the third phrase, and all sing the final phrase.

You are the Light of the World (2204)

Themes: Prayer; trust; hope

Michael Card has a wonderful ability of weaving a story with word and melody. One of his earlier songs is this simple chorus. In the text, Christ is shown as the light of the world, the bread of life, and the overcomer of the world. Each stanza also assures us of the hope that we find in Christ. This would be lovely sung with guitar accompaniment in an evening candlelight prayer service. If you have members of your congregation who are involved with the dramatic arts, have a soloist sing this song while your actors present a still life scene interpreting the text for each stanza. Interpretive dance or signing would enhance the presentation of this chorus. This song would also work well during Holy Communion.

You are worthy (2063)

Eres Digno

Themes: God's grace and power; God's reign; praise

This simple but beautiful song from Latin America reminds us of God's sovereignty and leads us to confess that God alone is worthy of all praise. It can be a response to prayer or to the Word. It can also be used as a response to "enthronement" psalms, such as Psalms 24, 47, 89:5-18, and 93. It is also appropriate during the season after Pentecost. Suggested tempo: ($\quarternote$ = 96).

You shall go out with joy (2279)
Themes: Second Coming; joy; provision and deliverance; closing of service

Send your congregation out into "the world" with this rousing benediction accompanied by drums, keyboard, tambourine, and hand claps. As the choir recesses and forms a circle around the congregation, have someone read Isaiah 55:12, from which the text is taken. Or, have the congregation read the scripture together in unison, then have the choir lead in singing the chorus as everyone is dismissed. Sing it at a moderate tempo at first, building speed on subsequent repetitions. The Singer's and Accompaniment Editions include an optional extended choral part for an exciting ending.

You who are thirsty (2132)
Themes: Invitation; comfort; encouragement; provision; communion; God's holiness

This song combines scripture references to invitation: Isaiah 55:1 and Matthew 11:28. A very fitting place in the service to use this song would be as a response to the scripture readings or at the end of the sermon. Teach it to the congregation earlier in the service or perhaps just before the service begins. Sing the first half of the song through once. Then, let the congregation echo back to you as you sing phrase by phrase. Next, teach the second half of the song in the same manner. Make a brief statement about the fulfillment and satisfaction that one finds when they bring their needs to Christ and sing the song through once more.

This song also works well as a musical invitation to communion. Have a soloist or choir sing this as the congregation moves orward to receive the elements. If your congregation sings as the elements are being served, use this song as one of the opening songs.

Your only Son (2113)
Themes: Christ's redemptive works; repentance and forgiveness; our love for God

The text of this song makes it appropriate for use anytime during Holy Week or Easter. It is beautiful as a solo, allowing for more *rubato* and a freer interpretation than would be possible with a congregation.

Soloists could sing the three stanzas with the congregation joining on the refrain. (Listen to a recording by Twila Paris.) It is possible to use this as a congregational song if a steady tempo is kept ($\quarternote$ = 60). Interpretive dance is very effective with this song. It is especially beautiful if interpreted by a solo dancer wearing solid white, representing the Lamb. At the conclusion of the song, the congregation could be invited to join in singing "O How He Loves You and Me" (2108). The accompanist would need to prepare a transition between the two songs.

ACKNOWLEDGMENTS

Use of copyrighted material is gratefully acknowledged by the publisher. Every effort has been made to locate the administrator of each copyright. The publisher would be pleased to have any errors or omissions brought to its attention. All copyright notices include the following declarations: All rights reserved. International copyright secured. Used with permission.

Abingdon Press (see The Copyright Company)
Above the Rim Music (ASCAP) (see BMG Songs, Inc.)
Acuff-Rose Music Publishing, Inc.; 65 Music Square, West; Nashville, TN 37203; (615) 321-5000; FAX 327-0560
Doris Akers (see Hal Leonard Corporation)
Albert E. Brumley & Sons (SESAC) (see Integrated Copyright Group). "I'll Fly Away" in *Wonderful Message* by Hartford Music Co.
Alfred Publishing Co., Inc.; 16320 Roscoe Blvd.; Van Nuys, CA 91410-0003; (818) 891-5999
Anglican Church of Canada; 600 Jarvis St.; Toronto, ON M4Y 2J6 (416) 924-9199x277; FAX (416) 924-0211; glight@national.anglican.ca
Ariose Music (ASCAP) (see EMI Christian Music Group)
Augsburg Fortress Publishers; P.O. Box 1209; Minneapolis, MN 55440-1209; (612) 330-3300
Birdwing Music (ASCAP) (see EMI Christian Music Group)
BMG Songs (ASCAP) (see EMI Christian Music Group)
BMG Songs, Inc. (ASCAP) 1400 18th Ave., S.; Nashville, TN 37212; (615) 858-1300
Boosey & Co., Ltd. (see Boosey & Hawkes, Inc.)
Boosey & Hawkes, Inc.; 24 East 21st St.; New York, NY 10010
Brentwood-Benson Music Publishing, Inc. (ASCAP); Attn: Copyright Administration; 741 Cool Springs Blvd.; Franklin, TN 37067

Brier Patch Music; 4324 Canal Southwest; Grandville, MI 49418; (616) 534-1113 (FAX)
Broadman Press (see Van Ness Press, Inc.)
Bud John Songs, Inc. (ASCAP) (see EMI Christian Music Group)
Carol Joy Music (ASCAP) (see Integrated Copyright Group)
Celebration (see The Copyright Company)
Chalice Press; Christian Board of Publication; 1316 Convention Plaza; Box 179; St. Louis, MO 63166-0179; (800) 366-3383; FAX (314) 231-2027; curriculum@cbp21.com
Changing Church Forum; 200 E. Nicollet Blvd.; Burnsville, MN 55337; (800) 874-2044; FAX (612) 435-8015
Skinner Chávez-Melo; c/o Juan Francisco Chávez-Melo; Juarez no. 85 Casa 19; Col. Ampliacion Miguel Hidalgo; Tlalpan 14250; Mexico D. F. Mexico; (011) 525-528-1884; chavezme@prodigy.net.mx
Susan Palo Cherwien (see Augsburg Fortress Publishers)
Choristers Guild; 2834 W. Kingsley Rd.; Garland, TX 75041-2498; (972) 271-1521; FAX (972) 840-3113
Church Publishing, Inc.; 445 Fifth Ave.; New York, NY 10016; (212) 592-1800x360; FAX (212) 779-3392
J. Jefferson Cleveland (see William B. McClain)
Cokesbury (see The Copyright Company)
Common Cup Co.; 7591 Gray Ave.; Burnby BC V5J 3ZY; (604) 434-8323
Concionero Abierto; c/o Pablo Sosa; Eparlaco 634; 1406 Buenos Aires, Argentina

Concordia Publishing House; 3558 South Jefferson Ave; St. Louis, MO 63118-3968; (314) 268-1000; FAX (314) 268-1329; www.cph.org
Damean Music (see GIA Publications, Inc.)
Dayspring Music, Inc. (BMI) (see Acuff-Rose Music Publishing, Inc.)
Desert Flower Music; P.O. Box 1476; Carmichael, CA 95609; (916) 481-2999
Andrew Donaldson; 14 Hambly Ave.; Toronto, Ontario M4E 2R6; (416) 691-1158; FAX: (416) 690-9967; seraph@pathcom.com
Doubleday; 1540 Broadway; New York, NY 10036; (212) 782-8957; FAX (212) 782-8898
Dr. Margaret P. Douroux; Rev. Earl Pleasant Publishing; P.O. Box 3247; Thousand Oaks, CA 91359; (818) 991-3728; FAX (818) 991-2567; GospelMeg@aol.com
Delores Dufner (see OCP Publications)
Earthsongs; 220 NW 29th St.; Corallis, OR 97330
E.C. Schirmer; 138 Ipswich St.; Boston, MA 02215
EMI Christian Music Group; P.O. Box 5085; 101 Winners Circle; Brentwood, TN 37024-5085; (615) 371-4300
Ever Devoted Music (see The Copyright Company)
Stanley M. Farr; 518 Fairmont Rd.; Morgantown, WV 26505
F.E.L. Publications (see The Lorenz Corporation)
Fred Bock Music Co., Inc.; 18345 Ventura Blvd., Suite 212; Tarzana, CA 91356; (618) 996-6181; FAX (618) 996-2043
Gaither Copyright Management; P.O. Box 737; Alexandria, IN 46001; (765) 724-8233; FAX (765) 724-8290

Gamut Music Productions; 704 Saddle Trail Ct.; Hermitage, TN 37076

Steve Garnaas-Holmes; 20 Greenbrier Dr.; Missoula, MT 59802

General Board of Global Ministries, GBGMusik; 475 Riverside Dr.; Room 350; New York, NY 10115 (print licenses 2109 and 2095)

GIA Publications, Inc.; 7404 S. Mason Ave.; Chicago, IL 60638; (800) GIA-1358; FAX (708) 496-3828

Hal Leonard Corp.; 777 W. Bluemound Rd.; Milwaukee, WI 53213

Marilyn Houser Hamm; Box 1887; Altona, Manitoba; Canada R0G 0B0; FAX (204) 831-5675

Harold Flammer, Inc.; 49 Waring Dr.; Delaware Water Gap, PA 18327-0690; FAX (717) 476-5247

Harper Collins Religious (see The Copyright Company)

Carl Haywood; 5228 Foxboro Landing; Virginia Beach, VA 23464 (757) 467-8971; FAX (757) 467-2172

Heart of the City Music; 300 E. Main St.; Anoka, MN 55503; (612) 323-4361

Hillsongs Publishing (ASCAP) (see Integrity's Hosanna! Music)

Hinshaw Music, Inc.; P.O. Box 470; Chapel Hill, NC 27514-0470; (919) 933-1691; FAX (919) 967-3399

Hodder and Stoughton Limited; 338 Euston Rd.; London, NW1 3BH, England; FAX 020-787-36308

Hope Publishing Company; 380 S. Main Pl.; Carol Stream, IL 60188; (800) 323-1049; FAX (630) 665-2552; www.hopepublishing.com

House of Mercy Music (see The Copyright Company)

Jane Parker Huber (see Westminster John Knox Press)

Coni Huisman; 3239 Tettis Ave., NE; Ada, MI 49301

Integrated Copyright Group; P.O. Box 24149; Nashville, TN 37202

Integrity Music, Inc.; 1000 Cody Rd.; Mobile, AL 36695-3425; (334) 633-9000; FAX (334) 633-9998

Integrity's Hosanna! Music (ASCAP); c/o Integrity Music, Inc.; 1000 Cody Rd.; Mobile, AL 36695-3425; (334) 633-9000; FAX (334) 633-9998

John T. Benson Publishing Co. (ASCAP) (see Brentwood-Benson Music Publishing, Inc.)

Jonathan Mark Music (ASCAP) (see EMI Christian Music Group)

Jubilate Hymns (see Hope Publishing Company)

Juniper Landing Music (see Word Music)

Kingsway's Thank You Music (see EMI Christian Music Group)

Ron Klusmeier; 345 Pym St.; Parksville, B.C., Canada V9P 1C8; (250) 954-2319; FAX (250) 954-1683; staff@musik-lus.com

Latter Rain Music (ASCAP) (see EMI Christian Music Group)

Geonyong Lee; c/o St. Paul Church; 2-20-1 Megura, Gohonggi; Tokyo, Japan 153-0053; FAX 82-2-520-8109

Les Presses de Taizé (see GIA Publications, Inc.)

Lillenas Publishing Company (see The Copyright Company)

Lilly Mack Music (BMI); 421 E. Beach; Inglewood, CA 90302; (310) 677-5603; FAX (310) 677-0250

Lutheran Book of Worship (see Augsburg Fortress Publishers)

Lynn C. Franklin Associates, Ltd.; 1350 Broadway, Suite 2015; New York, NY 10018; (212) 868-6311; FAX (212) 868-6312; lcf@fsainc.com

William B. McClain; c/o The Estate of J. Jefferson Cleveland; 4500 Massachusetts Ave., NW; Washington, D.C. 20016

Make Way Music (see Music Services, Inc.)

James K. Manley; Music by Jim Manley; 690 Persian Dr., #67; Sunnyvale, CA 94089; (408) 747-0667; jmanley@aol.com

Maranatha! Music (see The Copyright Company)

Maranatha Praise, Inc. (see The Copyright Company)

Martin and Morris (see Hal Leonard Corporation)

Matters Most Music (ASCAP) (see Brentwood-Benson Music Publishing, Inc.)

Meadowgreen Music Company (ASCAP) (see EMI Christian Music Group)

Mercy/Vineyard Publishing (see Music Services, Inc.)

Mole End Music (see Brentwood-Benson Music Publishing, Inc.)

Mountain Spring Music (ASCAP) (see EMI Christian Music Group)

Music Services, Inc. (ASCAP); 209 Chapelwood Dr.; Franklin, TN 37069; (615) 794-9015; FAX (615) 794-0793; www.musicservices.org

New Song Creations; R.R. 1, Box 454; Erin, TN 37061

New Spring Publishing, Inc. (ASCAP) (see Brentwood-Benson Music Publishing, Inc.)

Fintan O'Carroll (see OCP Publications)

OCP Publications; Attn: Licensing Dept.; P.O. Box 18030; Portland, OR 97218-0030; (800) 548-8749; FAX (503) 282-3486; liturgy@ocp.org ("Make Me a Channel of Your Peace" is dedicated to Mrs. Frances Tracy)

Oxford University Press; Great Clarendon St.; Oxford OX2 6DP, UK; 441-865-267254; FAX 441-865-267749

Oxford University Press, Inc.; 198 Madison Ave.; New York, NY 10016-4314; (212) 726-6000; FAX (212) 726-6444

Palm Branch Music, Inc.; 5808 Kimisu Ln.; Richmond, TX; (281) 344-9899; (281) 242-5174

Pamela Kay Music (ASCAP) (see EMI Christian Music Group)

Pilot Point Music (see The Copyright Company)

Prism Tree Music (see The Lorenz Corporation)

John S. Rice; Estate of John S. Rice; c/o Brian H. Davidson, Executor; 10619 Alameda Dr.; Knoxville, TN 37392-2502

River Oaks Music Company (BMI) (see EMI Christian Music Group)

ROM Administration; P.O. Box 1252; Fairhope, AL 36533; (334) 929-2411; FAX (334) 929-2404

Julian B. Rush; 1433 Williams St.; Unit 302; Denver, CO 80218-2531; (303) 837-0166x101; FAX (303) 837-9213

Taihei Sato; 9-2-20-1402 Takashimadaira; Habushi-ku; Tokyo 175; Japan

Scripture in Song (ASCAP) (see Integrity Music, Inc.)

Selah Publishing Co. Inc.; 58 Pearl St.; Kingston, NY 12402; (914) 338-2816; FAX (914) 338-2991; www.selah-pub.com

Shepherd's Fold Music (BMI) (see EMI Christian Music Group)

Singspiration Music (ASCAP) (see Brentwood-Benson Music Publishing, Inc.)

Songchannel Music Co. (ASCAP) (see EMI Christian Music Group)

SongWard Music (see Brentwood-Benson Music Publishing, Inc.)

Sound III, Inc. (see Universal-MCA Music Publishing)

Sovereign Music UK; P.O. Box 356; Leighton Buzzard, Beds. LU7 8WP UK; 44-1-525-385578; FAX 44-1-525-372743; SovereignM@aol.com

Leo Sowerby; Ronald Stalford, Executor; Estate of Leo Sowerby; 136 Coolidge Rd.; Worcester, MA 01602

Stainer & Bell Ltd. (see Hope Publishing Co.)

Linda Stassen (see New Song Creations)

Straightway Music (ASCAP) (see EMI Christian Music Group)

The American Lutheran Church (see Augsburg Fortress Publishers)

The Church Pension Fund (see Church Publishing, Inc.)

The Copyright Company; 40 Music Square, East; Nashville, TN 37203; FAX (615) 244-5591

The Hymn Society (see Hope Publishing Company)

The Kruger Organization, Inc.; 4501 Connecticut Ave., NW; Suite 711; Washington, DC 20008; (202) 966-3280; FAX (202) 364-1367

The Lorenz Corporation; 501 East Third St.; Dayton, OH 45402-2118; (937) 228-6118; FAX (937) 223-2042; info@Lorenz.com

The Pilgrim Press; 700 Prospect Ave., E.; Cleveland, OH 44115

The United Methodist Publishing House (see The Copyright Company)

ThreeFold Amen Music (see ROM Administration)

John D. Thornburg; 1211 Preston Rd.; Dallas, TX 75230; (214) 363-2479; FAX (214) 373-3972

Desmond Tutu (see Lynn C. Franklin Associates, Ltd.)

Unichappell Music, Inc. (see Hal Leonard Corporation)

Universal-MCA Music Publishing (see Warner Bros. Publications U.S., Inc.)

Universal-PolyGram International Publishing, Inc. (see Warner Bros. Publications U.S., Inc.)

Utryck (see Walton Music Corporation)

Utterbach Music, Inc. (see Warner Bros. Publications U.S., Inc.)

Van Ness Press, Inc.; FAX (615) 251-2869

Christopher Walker (see OCP Publications)

Mary Lu Walker; 16 Brown Rd.; Corning, NY 14830; (607) 936-4801; marluwalk@aol.com

William L. Wallace; 215A Mt. Pleasant Rd.; Christchurch, New Zealand; FAX +64 3 3840111

Walton Music Corporation; P.O. Box 167; Bynum, NC 27228; (919) 542-5548; FAX (919) 542-5527; writeus@waltonmusic.com

Warner Bros. Publications U.S., Inc.; 15800 Northwest 48th Ave.; Miami, FL 33014

Westminster John Knox Press; 100 Witherspoon St.; Louisville, KY 40202-1396; (502) 569-5342; FAX (502) 569-5113 ("Wonder of Wonders" is from *A Singing Faith*)

WGRG (See GIA Publications, Inc.)

Wendell Whalum; The Estate of Wendell Whalum; c/o Clarie Whalum; 2439 Greenwood Cir.; East Point, GA 30344

Whole Armor/Full Armor Music (see The Kruger Organization, Inc.)

Willing Heart Music (see The Copyright Company)

Word Music (see Acuff-Rose Music Publishing, Inc.)

Word Music, Inc. (see Acuff-Rose Music Publishing, Inc.)

John Ylvisaker; Box 321; Waverly, IA 50677

Darlene Zschech (ASCAP) (see Integrity's Hosanna! Music)

METRICAL INDEX

How to Use the Metrical Index

At the bottom right-hand corner of the first page of each song is the **tune name** (in small capital letters, such as BEACH SPRING) and **meter** (a series of numbers or letters, such as 87.87 D). The meter of a hymn or song indicates the number of syllables in each line of the text. For example, the meter of the first hymn in this collection, "We Sing to You, O God," is 66.66.88. The meter indicates that first four lines of the text have six syllables each, and the last two phrases have eight syllables.

Some meters have numerical designations, such as the example stated above. Others are so common that they have abbreviated names. Common meter (CM) is 86.86. Long meter (LM) is 88.88. Short meter (SM) is 66.86. The D following any meter indicates that it is doubled, such as CMD or 86.86 D to indicate 86.86.86.86. Some hymns have a refrain added to the text of the hymn, so their meters will indicate this by including the phrase "with refrain" after the meter (CMD with refrain). Other meters have no consistent pattern of syllables and are called irregular meter.

The meter designation becomes especially helpful when a particular hymn text is set to an unfamiliar tune. Using this metrical index, you may find a more familiar tune that will fit the text you wish to sing. First, determine the meter of the text you wish to use by looking at the bottom right-hand corner of the first page of the song (under the tune name). Then, look in the index for that particular meter (the meters are organized alphabetically and then numerically). There will be a list of tunes in the Supplement with the same meter. Check the other tunes for ones that are more familiar to your congregation. You might also check the metrical index in *The United Methodist Hymnal* for other familiar tunes. Once you find a tune that is familiar, sing the words to the text you wish to use to the new tune to make sure the words actually fit. Some meters may be the same, but the emphasis of the words or the nature of the tune may not fit the text you wish to use.

Changing the tune of a hymn is not a substitute for learning new hymn tunes. However, it does allow the new and appropriate hymn texts to be sung when there is no opportunity to learn a new tune.

CM (86.86)
CRIMOND   2181
LAND OF REST   2241
MARTYRDOM   2196
MORNING SONG   2180

CM with Refrain
GLASER   2242
WHISTLER'S TUNE   2097

CMD (86.86 D)
KINGSFOLD   2137, 2216, 2246
RESIGNATION   2182

CMD with Refrain
LEAVE ALL THINGS BEHIND   2101

LM (88.88)
AFTER THE FALL   2135
DIGNO   2063
FIRST HAND   2094

GIFT OF LOVE   2076
MARYTON   2050
O WALY WALY   2027, 2283
POXON   2185
PENTECOST   2247
PROSPECT   2052
PUER NOBIS NASCITUR   2121
WHEN JESUS WEPT   2106

LM with Refrain
BREAD OF PEACE   2255

SM (66.86)
BEAUTIFUL   2064
TWENTY   2245

37.65 D 3
STANISLAUS   2178

448.448
INTO MY HEART   2160

45.45 with Refrain
STAR CHILD   2095

4.77 with Refrain
DAWN   2210

4.74.74
CONFESIÓN   2134

54.54 D
KINDRED   2225
WELCOME SONG   2265

55.11 D
SAN ANSELMO   2175

55.54 D
BUNESSAN   2166, 2248
EARTH PRAYER   2059
EVENING HYMN   2187

METRICAL INDEX

CONTEMPORARY MEDLEYS

(Medleys using contemporary worship songs from *The Faith We Sing*)

SONG TITLE/NUMBER	KEY	MODULATION CHORDS
A. OPENING OF SERVICE		
Fast to Medium		
He Has Made Me Glad (2270)	D	
Clap Your Hands (2028)	D	Bm7 – Esus – E
Shout to the Lord (2074)	A	
Fast to Medium		
He Has Made Me Glad (2270)		D
We Bring the Sacrifice of Praise (2031)	D – E♭	E♭/D♭ – C7
Blessed Be the Name of the Lord (2034)		F
Fast to Medium		
My Life Is in You, Lord (2032)	G	
Lord, I Lift Your Name on High (2088)	G	
I Sing Praises to Your Name (2037)	G	
From the Rising of the Sun (2024)	G	
Fast to Medium		
I Will Call upon the Lord 2002	D	
Lord God, Almighty 2006	D	
All I Need Is You 2080	D	
Fast to Slow		
How Majestic Is Your Name (2023)	C	
Great Is the Lord (2022)	C	
Glorify Thy Name (2016)	C	
Holy, Holy (2039)	C (only)	direct segue
Sing Alleluia to the Lord (2258)	Cm	
Fast to Slow		
We Bring the Sacrifice of Praise (2031)	D – E♭	
Bless His Holy Name (2015)	E♭	E♭/D♭ – Csus – C
Blessed Be the Name of the Lord (2034)	F	
Honor and Praise (2018)	F	
Medium		
He Who Began a Good Work in You (2163)	G	direct segue
Humble Thyself in the Sight of the Lord (2131)	Em	
Awesome God (2040)	Em	

SONG TITLE/NUMBER	KEY	MODULATION CHORDS
Medium		
All Hail King Jesus (2069)	F	
Hosanna! Hosanna! (2109)	F	
He Is Exalted (2070)	F	
Jesus, Name Above All Names (2071)	F	

B. PRAISE AND WORSHIP

Medium		
Praise the Name of Jesus (2066)	C – D	Dsus7 – D7
I Sing Praises to Your Name (2037)		G
Jesus Be Praised (2079)	G	
Medium		
People Need the Lord (2244)	C	
Cares Chorus (2215)	C	
Lord, Listen to Your Children (2207)	C	
Medium to Slow		
Give Thanks (2036)	F	
Father, I Adore You (2038)	F	
More Precious than Silver (2065)	F	
Slow to Medium		
King of Kings and Lord of Lords (2075)	Em	
The King of Glory Comes (2091)	Em	Em7 – G/A – A7
We Will Glorify the King of Kings (2087)	D	
Slow to Medium		
Lord, Be Glorified (2150)	C (only)	
Make Us One (2224)	C	Am7 – Dsus – D
We Are the Body of Christ (2227)	G	
Slow		
Honor and Praise (2018)	F	
More Precious than Silver (2065)	F	
I Love You, Lord (2068)	F	
Slow		
O Lord, You're Beautiful (2064)	D	
Open Our Eyes, Lord (2086)	D	
As the Deer (2025)	D	
Slow		
O Lord, Your Tenderness (2143)	E♭	
Give Me a Clean Heart (2133)	E♭	Cm7 – Fsus – F
Water, River, Spirit, Grace (2253)	B♭	

SONG TITLE/NUMBER	KEY	MODULATION CHORDS
Slow		
In His Time (2203)	D	
Sanctuary (2164)	D – E♭	
O Lord, Your Tenderness (2143)	E♭	
Slow		
Change My Heart, O God (2152)	C	
Lord, Be Glorified (2150)	C – D	D7sus – D7
Make Me a Servant (2176)	G	

C. INVITATION (PRAYER/COMMITMENT)

Medium		
Please Enter My Heart, Hosanna (2154)	D	
Cry of My Heart (2165)	D	
Medium		
More Like You (2167)	B♭	B♭7sus – B♭7
To Know You More (2161)	E♭	E♭7sus – E♭7
The Family Prayer Song (2188)	A♭	
Medium to Slow		
Grace Alone (2162)	C	Am7 – Dsus – D
He Who Began a Good Work in You (2163)	G	Em7 – Asus – A
Sanctuary (2164)		

D. COMMUNION

Medium to Slow		
Come to the Table (2264)	F	Dm7 – Gsus - G
You Who Are Thirsty (2132)	C	
Holy, Holy (2039)	C – D♭	
Medium		
Here Is Bread, Here Is Wine (2266)	C – D	Dsus7 – D7
Come, Share the Lord (2269)	G	

E. CLOSING

Medium		
Make Us One (2224)	C	Am7 – Dsus – D
We Are the Body of Christ (2227)	G – A♭	direct segue
They'll Know We Are Christians by Our Love (2223)	Fm	
Medium		
Bind Us Together (2226)	F	
One God and Father of Us All (2240)	F	

BLENDED MEDLEYS

(Medleys using hymns and contemporary worship songs
from *The Faith We Sing* and *The United Methodist Hymnal*)

SONG TITLE/NUMBER	KEY	MODULATION CHORDS
A. OPENING OF SERVICE		
Fast		
I Will Enter His Gates (2270)	D	D/C – B♭
This Is the Day (UMH, 657)	E♭	
We Bring the Sacrifice of Praise (2031)	E♭ (only)	E♭/D♭ – Csus – C
Praise to the Lord, the Almighty (UMH, 139)	F	
Fast to Medium		
Celebrate Love (2073)	C	
Jesus Loves Me (UMH, 191)	C	
There's a Song (2141)	C	
Medium		
From the Rising of the Sun (2024)	G	
Praise to the Lord (2029)	G	
I Sing Praises to Your Name (2037)	G – A♭	
Medium		
O For a Thousand Tongues to Sing (UMH, 57)	G	
I Sing Praises to Your Name (2037)	G (only)	Em7 – Asus – A
We Sing to You, O God (2001)	D	
Medium		
Come, Let Us with Our Lord Arise (2084)	F	
This Is the Day the Lord Hath Made (UMH, 658)	F	
Praise the Lord with the Sound of Trumpet (2020)	F	
Medium to Slow		
Praise You (2003)	A – B♭	Gm7 – Csus – C7
More Precious than Silver (2065)	F	
Come and Find the Quiet Center (2128)	F	
B. PRAISE AND WORSHIP		
Fast		
Praise to the Lord, the Almighty (UMH, 139)	F	
Praise the Lord with the Sound of Trumpet (2020)	F	Dm7 – Gsus - G
How Majestic Is Your Name (2023)	C	
Fast to Medium		
All Creatures of Our God and King (UMH, 62)	E♭	
Now Thank We All Our God (UMH, 102)	E♭	direct segue
Praise Our God Above (2061)	Cm	

SONG TITLE/NUMBER	KEY	MODULATION CHORDS
Fast to Medium		
O Worship the King (UMH, 73)	G	
Come, Thou Almighty King (UMH, 61)	G	Em7 – Asus – A
We Will Glorify the King of Kings (2087)	D (only)	
Holy, Holy, Holy! Lord God Almighty (UMH, 64)	D	
Medium		
Bless His Holy Name (2015)	E♭	E♭7sus – E♭7
To God Be the Glory (UMH, 98)	A♭	
I Sing Praises to Your Name (2037)	A♭ (only)	
Medium		
He Who Began a Good Work in You (2163)	G	Em7 – Asus – A
Great Is Thy Faithfulness (UMH, 140)	D	
All I Need Is You (2080)	D – E	
Medium		
Praise You (2003)	A	Asus7 – A7
Lord, Be Glorified (2150)	D (only)	direct segue
Now Praise the Hidden God of Love (2027)	G	
Medium to Slow		
Let All Things Now Living (2008)	F	
Give Thanks (2036)	F	
Medium to Slow		
All Hail King Jesus (2069)	F	
Honor and Praise (2018)	F	
Jesus, Name Above All Names (2071)	F	
Slow		
Holy, Holy, Holy (2007)	C	
Holy, Holy (2039)	C (only)	
O God, Beyond All Praising (2009)	C	
Slow		
My Jesus, I Love Thee (UMH, 172)	F	
I Love You, Lord (2068)	F	
You Alone Are Holy (2077)	F	
Slow		
Lamb of God (2113)	C	Fm7 – E♭sus – E♭
O How He Loves You and Me (2108)	A♭	
O How I Love Jesus (UMH, 170 refrain)	A♭	

SONG TITLE/NUMBER	KEY	MODULATION CHORDS

C. INVITATION (PRAYER/COMMITMENT)

Medium

Into My Heart (2160)	F	Fsus – F7
More Like You (2167)	B♭	

Medium

I Have Decided to Follow Jesus (2129)	C	Am7 – Dsus – D
I'm Gonna Live So God Can Use Me (2153)	G	

Medium to Slow

What a Friend We Have in Jesus (UMH, 526)	F	
Turn Your Eyes upon Jesus (UMH, 349)	F	
Jesus, Draw Me Close (2159)	F	

Slow

Forgive Us, Lord (2134)	Dm	
Out of the Depths (2136)	Dm	direct segue
In His Time (2203)	D	
Sanctuary (2164)	D	

D. COMMUNION

Medium

Take Our Bread (UMH, 640)	C	Am7 – Dsus – D
All Who Hunger (2126)	G	
Eat This Bread (UMH, 628)	G	

Medium to Slow

Time Now to Gather (2265)	E♭	
Let Us Break Bread Together (UMH, 618)	E♭	
Holy Ground (2272)	E♭	

E. CLOSING

Medium

The Servant Song (2222)	E♭	E♭/D♭ – Csus – C7 – Fm
They'll Know We Are Christians by Our Love (2223)	Fm	direct segue
Bind Us Together (2226)	F	

Slow

Make Me a Servant (2176)	G	Em7 – Asus – A
Make Me a Channel of Your Peace (2171)	D	

BLENDED MEDLEYS BY TOPIC

(Medleys using hymns and contemporary worship songs from *The Faith We Sing*
and *The United Methodist Hymnal*)

SONG TITLE/NUMBER	KEY	MODULATION CHORDS
Assurance		
Blessed Assurance (369)	D	D/C – B♭
Oh, I Know the Lord's Laid His		
Hands on Me (2139)	E♭	E♭7 – D – D7
I've Got Peace Like a River (2145)	G	
Comfort		
Cares Chorus (2215)	C	C/B♭ – A♭sus – A♭7
It Is Well with My Soul (377)	D♭	D♭7 – Csus – C7
I Will Trust in the Lord (464)	F	
You Are My Hiding Place (2055)	F	
Communion, Holy*		
Holy, Holy, Holy (2007)	C	
O God Beyond All Praising (2009)	C	C/B♭ – Asus – A7
Great Is Thy Faithfulness (140)	D	
Holy, Holy, Holy! Lord God Almighty (64)	D	D7
Eat This Bread (628)	G	Gm7 – Fsus – F7
Let Us Be Bread (2260)	B♭	Gm7 – Csus – C7
Spirit of the Living God (393)	F	Dm7 – Gsus – G7
Make Us One (2224)	C	Am7 – Dsus – D7
Soon and Very Soon (706)	G	

*Based on the Great Thanksgiving Prayer, used during the serving of the elements

Communion, Holy**		
Let Us Break Bread Together (618)	E♭	E♭/D♭ – Csus – C7
I Come with Joy (vv. 1-3) (617)	F	F/E♭ – Dsus – D7
Be Present at Our Table, Lord (621)	G	
All Who Hunger (2126)	G	
One Bread, One Body (620)	G	G7
Here Is Bread, Here Is Wine (2266)	C	
Take Our Bread (640)	C	
Lord, Be Glorified (2150)	C	C7
I Come with Joy (vv. 4-5) (617)	F	

**Used during the serving of the elements

Confession, Pardon, and Assurance		
Change My Heart, O God (2152)	C	
Kyrie (2275)	C – D♭	
Lord, I Want to Be a Christian (402)	D♭	D♭/C♭ – Asus – A7
Blessed Assurance (369)	D	

SONG TITLE/NUMBER	KEY	MODULATION CHORDS
Eternal Life		
Joy in the Morning (2284)	Fm	Fm/E♭ – Dsus – D7
I'll Fly Away (2282)	G	
Soon and Very Soon (706)	G	
Sing with All the Saints in Glory (702)	G	
Evening		
From the Rising of the Sun (2024)	G	
Now It is Evening (2187)	G	
All Praise to Thee, My God, This Night (682)	G	
Global Praise		
Praise, Praise, Praise the Lord (2035)	C	C7
Alleluia (Honduras) (2078)	F	F/E♭ – Dsus – D7
Halle, Halle, Halleluja (2026)	G	
Glory		
To God Be the Glory (98)	A♭	A♭/G♭ – Esus – E7
Shine, Jesus Shine (2173)	A	A/G – Fsus – F7
My Tribute (99)	B♭	B♭/A♭ – Gsus – G7
Glorify Thy Name (2016)	C	
Gospel Songs		
The Lily of the Valley (2062)	F	F/E♭ – Dsus – D7
I'll Fly Away (2282)	G	G/F – Esus – E7
Since Jesus Came into My Heart (2140)	A	
Gratitude		
Give Thanks (2036)	F	F/E♭ – Dsus – D7
For the Beauty of the Earth (92)	G	Am7 – B♭sus – B♭7
Now Thank We All Our God (102)	E♭	
Healing		
Healer of Our Every Ill (2213)	D	
O Lord, You're Beautiful (2064)	D	D/C – B♭sus – B♭7
There Is a Balm in Gilead (375)	E♭	
Holy Spirit		
Come, Holy Spirit (2125)	C	C/B♭ – Asus – A7
Spirit, Spirit of Gentleness (2120)	D	
Surely the Presence of the Lord (328)	D	D/C – B♭sus – B♭7
Spirit of the Living God (393)	E♭	
Hope		
All I Need Is You (2080)	D – E	E/D – Csus – C7
My Hope Is Built (368)	F	
Amazing Grace (378)	F	

SONG TITLE/NUMBER	KEY	MODULATION CHORDS
Kingdom of God		
I Love Thy Kingdom, Lord (540)	F	Gm7 – Asus – A7
Bring Forth the Kingdom (2190)	D	
Rejoice, the Lord Is King (715)	D	
Light		
We Are Marching (2235-b)	G	G7
Light of the World (2204)	C	Dm7 – Esus – E7
Shine, Jesus, Shine (2173)	A	
Love of God through Jesus		
O Lord, Your Tenderness (2143)	E♭	E♭7
O How He Loves You And Me (2108)	A♭	
Because He Lives (364)	A♭	
Name of Jesus		
I Sing Praises to Your Name (2037)	G (only)	G7
Praise the Name of Jesus (2066)	C – D	D/C – B♭sus – B♭7
There's Something About That Name (171)	E♭	E♭/D – Csus – C7
Jesus, Name Above All Names (2071)	F	
All Hail the Power of Jesus' Name (154)	F	
His Name Is Wonderful (174)	F	Dm7 – Gsus – G7
How Majestic Is Your Name (2023)	C	
Peace		
Make Me a Channel of Your Peace (2171)	D	Dm7 – Gsus – G7
Let There Be Peace on Earth (431)	C	C7
Dona Nobis Pacem (376)	F	
Salvation		
Victory in Jesus (370)	G	
Lord, I Lift Your Name on High (2088)	G	G/F – E♭sus – E♭7
I'm So Glad Jesus Lifted Me (2151)	A♭	A♭/G – Esus – E7
Since Jesus Came into My Heart (2140)	A	
Service		
Living For Jesus (2149)	F	direct segue
They'll Know We Are Christians by Our Love (2223)	Fm	Fm7 – Gsus – G7
Lord, Be Glorified (2150)	C	
Testimony and Witness		
Marching to Zion (733)	G	G/F – E♭sus – E♭7
O How I Love Jesus (170)	A♭	
I'm So Glad Jesus Lifted Me (2151)	A♭	A♭/G♭ – Esus – E7
Since Jesus Came Into My Heart (2140)	A	

SONG TITLE/NUMBER	KEY	MODULATION CHORDS
Trinity		
Glorify Thy Name (2016)	C	
Holy, Holy (2039)	C-D♭	D♭/C♭ – Asus – A7
Holy, Holy, Holy! Lord God Almighty (64)	D	Dm7 – Csus – C7
Father, I Adore You (2038)	F	
Unity		
We Are One in Christ Jesus (2229)	Em	Em/D – Csus – C7
Bind Us Together (2226)	F	G7
Make Us One (2224)	C	

MODULATION FORMULAS

Raising the key by a half step or a whole step between the final two stanzas of a hymn can be an "uplifting" worship experience. The keyboard player may insert a short original modulation between the last two stanzas, but this requires a high degree of creativity and craftsmanship, and a keen sense of the timing of such an interlude.

An easier method of modulation is as follows:

In the last measure of penultimate stanzas,

1. On the second beat, move the bass note down one whole step if modulating up one half step, or down one half step if modulating up one whole step, holding the upper voices;

2. On the next beat, move the bass note down an additional whole step, at the same time moving the upper voices to the dominant chord of the new key;

3. Finally, add the 7th to this dominant chord, and, if needed, change its position to lead naturally to the opening melodic note of the final stanza.

The following examples illustrate these formulas in 4/4 and 3/4 meters, and with the first melody note beginning on the root, third, and fifth notes of the new key.

Half-Step Modulations

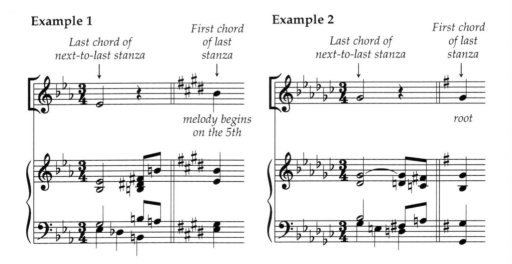

Example 1

Last chord of next-to-last stanza

First chord of last stanza

melody begins on the 5th

Example 2

Last chord of next-to-last stanza

First chord of last stanza

root

Example 3

Last chord of
next-to-last stanza

First chord
of last
stanza

3rd

Example 4

Last chord of
next-to-last stanza

First chord
of last
stanza

3rd

Whole-Step Modulations

Example 5

Last chord of
next-to-last stanza

First chord
of last
stanza

melody begins
on the 5th

Example 6

Last chord of
next-to-last stanza

First chord
of last
stanza

root

Example 7

Last chord of
next-to-last stanza

First chord
of last
stanza

3rd

Example 8

Last chord of
next-to-last stanza

First chord
of last
stanza

3rd

INDEX OF TUNE NAMES

How to Use the Tune Name Index

At the bottom right-hand corner of the first page of each song is the **tune name** (in capital letters, such as BEACH SPRING) and **meter** (a series of numbers or letters, such as 87.87 D). The tune name is the name that has been given to this particular hymn tune. The meter of a hymn or song indicates the number of syllables in each line of the text.

Some hymn tunes are written in common meters, and therefore may be used with a number of different hymn texts. Other hymn tunes are written to a particular hymn text and cannot be used with any other text.

This index may be used with the metrical index when you are looking for a familiar hymn tune for a new hymn text. In addition, with this index you can determine if there are some new hymn texts set to tunes your congregation knows.

INDEX OF KEYS

[K–K] = beginning–ending keys
[K(–K)] = beginning key–optional ending key (or chord)

D Minor

E♭ Major

G Minor

INDEX OF SCRIPTURE

INDEX OF TOPICS AND CATEGORIES

Lent 2108-2113, 2126-2138, 2155-2168. *Also:*
2152 Change my heart, O God
2105 Jesus, tempted in the desert
2106 When Jesus wept
2089 Wild and lone the prophet's voice
2055 You are my hiding place

Passion/Palm Sunday
2109 *Hosanna! Hosanna!*
2083 My song is love unknown
2091 The King of glory comes
2111 We sang our glad hosannas
2087 We will glorify the King of kings

Holy Week 2108-2113. *Also:*
2254 In remembrance of me (Maundy Thursday)
2176 Make me a servant (Maundy Thursday)
2083 My song is love unknown
2106 When Jesus wept
2077 You alone are holy (*Sólo Tú Eres Santo*)

Easter 2114-2116. *Also:*
2078 Alleluia (Honduras)
2084 Come, let us with our Lord arise
2070 He is exalted
2077 You alone are holy (*Sólo Tú Eres Santo*)

Mother's Day
2189 A mother lined a basket
2050 Mothering God, you gave me birth

Pentecost 2117-2125. *Also:*
2142 *Blessed Quietness*
2019 Holy (*Santo*)
2193 Lord, listen to your children praying
2241 The Spirit sends us forth to serve
2220 We are God's people
2229 We are one in Christ Jesus (*Somos Uno en Cristo*)
2077 You alone are holy (*Sólo Tú Eres Santo*)

Trinity Sunday. *See* **Trinity**

Christ the King (Reign of Christ)
2069 All hail King Jesus
2070 He is exalted
2284 *Joy in the Morning*

2075 King of Kings and Lord of lords
2091 The King of glory comes
2087 We will glorify the King of kings
2063 You are worthy (*Eres Digno*)

All Saints Day
2155 Blest are they
2283 For all the saints
2042 How lovely, Lord, how lovely
2224 Make us one, Lord
2229 We are one in Christ Jesus (*Somos Uno en Cristo*)

Thanksgiving Day
2271 Come! Come! Everybody worship (*Vengan Todos Adoremos*)
2036 Give thanks with a grateful heart
2059 I am your mother
2008 Let all things now living
2044 My gratitude now accept, O God (*Gracias, Señor*)
2061 Praise our God above

CHURCH

Anniversaries
2221 In unity we lift our song
2220 We are God's people
2001 We sing to you, O God

The Bible: the Book of the Church
2246 Deep in the shadows of the past
2221 In unity we lift our song

Community in Christ 2220-2233. *Also:*
2236 *Gather Us In*
2273 Jesus, we are here (*Jesu, Tawa Pano*)
2179 Live in charity (*Ubi Caritas*)
2027 Now praise the hidden God of love
2240 *One God and Father of Us All*
2175 Together we serve
2243 We all are one in mission
2181 We need a faith

Dedication of a Building
2272 *Holy Ground*
2221 In unity we lift our song
2220 We are God's people

2050 Mothering God, you gave me birth
2054 Nothing can trouble (*Nada Te Turbe*)
2018 *Honor and Praise*
2233 *Where Children Belong*
2225 Who is my mother, who is my brother?
2132 You who are thirsty

CONFESSION. *See* **Service Music**

CONFIRMATION. *See* **Commitment.** *Also:*
2170 God made from one blood
2060 God the sculptor of the mountains
2076 O blessed spring
2004 Praise the source of faith and learning

COURAGE. *See* **Strength and Courage**

CREATION 2059-2061. *Also:*
2008 Let all things now living
2012 Let us with a joyful mind
2020 Praise the Lord with the sound of trumpet
2004 Praise the source of faith and learning
2010 Praise ye the Lord
2228 Sacred the body
2122 She comes sailing on the wind
2074 Shout to the Lord
2120 Spirit, Spirit of gentleness
2041 Thou art worthy

CROSS OF JESUS. *See* **Jesus Christ**

DEDICATION OF A BUILDING. *See* **Church**

DISCIPLESHIP AND SERVICE 2155-2190. *Also:*
2239 Go ye, go ye into the world
2131 Humble thyself in the sight of the Lord
2129 I have decided to follow Jesus
2153 I'm gonna live so God can use me
2214 Lead me, guide me
2260 Let us be bread
2027 Now praise the hidden God of love
2102 Swiftly pass the clouds of glory
2241 The Spirit sends us forth to serve
2130 *The Summons*
2101 Two fishermen

2107 Wade in the water
2225 Who is my mother, who is my brother?
2089 Wild and lone the prophet's voice
2245 Within the day-to-day
2137 Would I have answered when you called

DOXOLOGIES. *See* **Service Music**

EARTH AND ENVIRONMENT
2060 God the sculptor of the mountains
2048 God weeps
2059 I am your mother
2061 Praise our God above
2041 Thou art worthy

EASTER. *See* **Christian Year**

ECUMENISM. *See* **Church**

EDUCATION. *See* **Church**

EPIPHANY. *See* **Christian Year**

ETERNAL LIFE 2282-2284
2192 *Freedom Is Coming*
2210 Joy comes with the dawn
2076 O blessed spring
2194 O freedom (African American spiritual)

EVENING
2187 Now it is evening
2205 *The Fragrance of Christ*

EXAMPLE OF JESUS. *See* **Jesus Christ**

FAITH
2189 A mother lined a basket
2215 *Cares Chorus*
2211 Faith is patience in the night
2203 In his time
2171 Make me a channel of your peace
2032 My life is in you, Lord
2054 Nothing can trouble (*Nada Te Turbe*)
2147 There are some things I may not know
2141 There's a song
2183 Unsettled world
2181 We need a faith
2196 We walk by faith

INDEX OF COMPOSERS, ARRANGERS, AUTHORS, TRANSLATORS, AND SOURCES

(A=Accompaniment Edition; Sg=Singer's Edition; Sm=Simplified Edition)

INDEX OF FIRST LINES AND COMMON TITLES

(Suggested tempo in parentheses.)

I

2158 I am weak, but thou art strong (♩ = 68)

2059 I am your mother (♩ = 108)

2215 I cast all my cares upon you (♩ = 88)

2129 I have decided to follow Jesus
(♩ = 64-76)

2062 I have found a friend in Jesus (♩ = 88-96)

2068 I love you, Lord (♩ = 96-104)

2037 I sing praises to your name (♩ = 92)

2094 I sought him dressed in finest clothes
(♩ = 104-112)

2051 I was there to hear your borning cry
(♩ = 96)

2002 I will call upon the Lord (♩ = 116)

2218 I will come to you in the silence
(♩ = 80-88)

2270 I will enter his gates (♩ = 116)

2053 If it had not been for the Lord (♩ = 88)

2282 *I'll Fly Away*

2153 I'm gonna live so God can use me
(♩ = 144)

2151 I'm so glad Jesus lifted me (♩ = 84)

2203 In his time (♩ = 84-92)

2150 In our lives, Lord, be glorified (♩ = 84)

2254 In remembrance of me (♩ = 92)

2195 In the Lord I'll be ever thankful (♩ = 80)

2238 In the midst of new dimensions
(♩ = 102)

2255 In the singing, in the silence (𝅗𝅥 = 56-60)

2221 In unity we lift our song (♩ = 92-100)

2160 Into my heart (♩ = 100)

2165 It is the cry of my heart (♩ = 100)

2145 I've got peace like a river (♩ = 124-132)

2250 I've just come from the fountain (♩ = 84)

J

2273 *Jesu, Tawa Pano*

2079 *Jesus Be Praised*

2159 Jesus, draw me close (♩ = 88-96)

2071 Jesus, name above all names (♩. = 66)

2109 Jesus rode into Jerusalem (♩ = 128-144)

2105 Jesus, tempted in the desert (𝅗𝅥 = 76-88)

2112 Jesus walked this lonesome valley
(♩ = 120-132)

2273 Jesus, we are here (♩ = 126)

2079 Jesus, we worship you (♩ = 92)

2099 Joseph dearest, Joseph mine (♩. = 60)

2210 Joy comes with the dawn (♩ = 80-92)

2284 *Joy in the Morning*

2142 Joys are flowing like a river (♩ = 80)

2017 *Jubilate Servite*

2158 *Just a Closer Walk with Thee*

K

2075 King of kings and Lord of lords
(♩ = 176)

2127 *Kyrie*

2275 Kyrie (♩ = 76)

L

2113 *Lamb of God*

2214 Lead me, guide me (♩ = 88-96)

2234 Lead on, O cloud of Presence
(♩ = 104-112)

2008 Let all things now living (♩ = 108)

2260 Let us be bread (♩ = 108)

2262 Let us offer to the Father (♩. = 66)

2012 Let us with a joyful mind (♩ = 108)

2261 Life-giving bread (♩ = 132-144)

2204 *Light of the World*

2090 Light the Advent candle (♩ = 144)

2092 Like a child (♩ = 80)

2179 Live in charity (♩ = 72)

2149 Living for Jesus (♩ = 132)

2150 *Lord, Be Glorified*

2006 Lord God, Almighty (♩ = 92-100)

2277 Lord, have mercy (♩ = 52-56)

2088 Lord, I lift your name on high (♩ = 86)

2201 Lord, let your kingdom come (♩ = 96)

2207 *Lord, Listen to Your Children*

2193 Lord, listen to your children praying
(♩ = 68-72)

2205 Lord, may our prayer rise like incense
(𝅗𝅥 = 56-60)